ACTS

A Contextual Commentary

DELANO VINCENT PALMER

Extra MILE Innovators
Kingston, Jamaica W.I.

Copyright © 2020 by Delano Palmer

ISBN-13: 978-1-62676-612-9

ALL RIGHTS RESERVED
Without limiting the rights under copyright reserved above, no part of this publication may be reproduced, stored in or introduced into a retrieval system, or transmitted, in any form, or by any means (electronic, mechanical, photocopying, recording, or otherwise), without the prior contractual or written permission of the copyright owner of this work.

. . . . .

Published by
Extra MILE Innovators
54 Montgomery Avenue
Kingston 10. Jamaica W.I.
www.extramileja.com

Cover Design: Pro-designer, Olivia

AUTHOR CONTACT
For consultation and speaking engagements email delanopalmer@ymail.com for more information.

NOTES

Scripture quotations identified as JNT are from the Jamaica New Testament, copyright 2012 by the Bible Society of the West Indies. Used by permission. All rights reserved.

Scripture quotations identified NKJV are from the New King James Version of the Bible. Copyright © 1979, 1980, 1982, by Thomas Nelson, Inc., Publishers. Used by permission. All rights reserved.

Unless otherwise identified, Scripture quotations are from the HOLY BIBLE, NEW INTERNATIONAL VERSION; copyright © 1973, 1978, 1984, 2010 by the International Bible Society, and Biblica, Inc.™ Used by permission. All rights reserved worldwide.

Scripture quotations identified NRSV are from the New Revised Standard Version of the Bible, copyright 1989 by the Division of Christian Education of the National Council of Churches of Christ in the U.S.A. Used by permission. All rights reserved.

Scripture quotations identified NKJV are from the New King James Version of the Bible. Copyright © 1979, 1980, 1982, by Thomas Nelson, Inc., Publishers. Used by permission. All rights reserved.

Scripture quotations identified AV/KJV are from the King James Version of the Bible.

All quotations marked DV (Darby Version) are taken from John Nelson Darby, Holy Bible: A New Translation. London: Morrish, 1929.

All quotations marked NET are taken from the NETBible® copyright ©1996-2006 by Biblical Studies Press, L.L.C. www.bible.org All rights reserved.

Scripture quotations identified REB are from The Revised English Bible published jointly by the Oxford University Press and Cambridge University Press, 1989. All rights reserved.

To
Dotty my beloved,
and especially
DOMINO,
who loves us all with an everlasting *hesed*

ABBREVIATIONS

ABD — Anchor Bible Dictionary

AJET — African Journal of Evangelical Theology

BAG — Bauer, W., et al., eds. A Greek-English Lexicon of the New Testament and Other Early Christian Literature. Revised by F. W. Danker. Chicago: Chicago University Press, 1957

BDAG — Bauer, W., et al., eds. A Greek-English Lexicon of the New Testament and Other Early Christian Literature. Revised by F. W. Danker. Chicago: Chicago University Press, 2000

BDF — Blass, F., A. Debrunner, and R. Funk. A Greek Grammar of the New Testament and Other Early Christian Literature. Chicago: University Press, 1961

BT — Bible Translator

CGST — Caribbean Graduate school of Theology

CJET — Caribbean Journal of Evangelical Theology

CJRS	Caribbean Journal of Religious Studies
CUP	Cambridge University Press
DBI	Dictionary of Biblical Interpretation
DV	Darby Version
EB	Encyclopedia Britannica
EBC	The Expositor's Bible Commentary
EGT	The Expositor's Greek Testament
ET	The Expository Times
GAGNT	A Grammatical Analysis of the Greek NT
GELS	Greek-English Lexicon of the Septuagint
HE	Historia Ecclesiastica
Ibid ibidem	In the same place
ICC	International Critical Commentary
IVP	Intervarsity Press
JBL	Journal of Biblical Literature JBR Jamaica Baptist Reporter

JSNT	Journal for the Study of the New Testament
JTS	Journal of Theological Studies
JTS	Jamaica Theological Seminary
LN	J. P. Louw, and Eugene A. Nida, eds. Greek-English Lexicon of the New Testament Based on Semantic Domains. New York: United Bible Societies, 1988.
LXX	Septuagint
MMJH	Moulton and George Milligan. The Vocabulary of the Greek Testament. Grand Rapids: Eerdmans, 1930
NIDONTE	New International Dictionary of New Testament Theology and Exegesis
NTS	New Testament Studies
NovT	Novum Testamentum
UBS	United Bible Societies UBS4 Aland, Barbara, and Kurt Aland, Johannes Karavidopoulos, Carlo M. Martini, Bruce Metzger, K Elliger, W. Rudolph, eds. Biblia Sacra Utriusque Testamenti Editio Hebraica et Graeca. Stuttgart: Deutsche Bibelgesellshaft, 1994

UMI	University Microfilms Incorporated (ProQuest)
UPA	University Press of America
VE	Vox Evangelica
YUP	Yale University Press

PREFACE

The gospel of the Lord Jesus Christ the Messiah emerged from a religiously pluralistic society over nineteen centuries ago. Today the same gospel—the good news of God's salvific endeavor for human flourishing—finds itself once again in a pluralistic world that is much more complex than the Roman Empire in which it was first proclaimed. It was under threat then. It is still under threat today. The Book of Acts (as well as its companion volume which bears the narrator's name) represents a First-Century physician's response to questions concerning the efficacy of this Gospel to adequately address the human condition.

There were rumours of serious and dangerous endeavors to overturn the work of the Spirit of God in the lives of those who had embraced the new movement that later became the Way. How viable was this movement? And if the rumours about its struggles are true, how can it help the hapless? Luke's second volume gives clear and confident answers to these and other queries. So we are grateful to the Almighty for having preserved for us the Book of Acts which charts the progress of Christianity in the First Century.

Three other books have inspired the writing of this commentary: *The Spreading Flame* by F.F Bruce (who started from where Acts closed off and landed us in Twentieth Century Britain), and Dr Lloyd Cooke's *The Story of Jamaican Missions*, with the revealing subtitle *How the Gospel Went from Jamaica to the World*. If Dr Cooke traces the fire of God's purifying grace to the present century, the following essay returns to the First.

The other book bears the ambitious title, *The Book of Acts: A Concise Caribbean Commentary*. The least said about it the better.

Today, fifty percent of my countrymen claim to have a personal relationship with God through His Son Christ Jesus. What is regrettable is that very few (it appears) churches in the Caribbean have caught the Lukan vision of planting new churches that are self governing, self supporting, self theologizing, and self propagating, cross culturally. There are no easy answers to this dilemma. A big part of the problem, it seems to me, is that too many Christians are waiting for a divine call instead of responding to the Great Commission.

After all, a missionary (or apostle) is a child of God who gives a positive response to the divine mandate for world evangelization (Luke 24; Acts 1). With billions around the world who have not heard the Lukan gospel, we should once again petition the Lord of the harvest to send forth labourers into the vineyard ripe and ready to harvest (Acts).

TABLE OF CONTENTS

INTRODUCTION 1
CHAPTER 1 50
CHAPTER 2 61
CHAPTER 3 73
CHAPTER 4 79
CHAPTER 5 83
CHAPTER 6 87
CHAPTER 7 90
CHAPTER 8 93
CHAPTER 9 103
CHAPTER 10 109
CHAPTER 11 115
CHAPTER 12 119
CHAPTER 13 123
CHAPTER 14 127
CHAPTER 15 131
CHAPTER 16 145
CHAPTER 17 149
CHAPTER 18 153
CHAPTER 19 159
CHAPTER 20 163
CHAPTER 21 171
CHAPTER 22 177
CHAPTER 23 181
CHAPTER 24 185
CHAPTER 25 189
CHAPTER 26 193
CHAPTER 27 199
CHAPTER 28 203

APPENDIX 1. The Apostle Paul and the Church 211
APPENDIX 2. CAFU... 221
APPENDIX 3. Reflections on Theological Education 227
APPENDIX 4. God's Will.. 231
APPENDIX 5. The JNT and Acts 238
APPENDIX 6. Sabbath, Sunday and The Third Millenium .. 244
APPENDIX 7. Pentecost and the Bride............................... 250
APPENDIX 8. A Birthday Worth Celebrating 253
APPENDIX 9. Prima Inter Partes 257
APPENDIX 10. Luke's Christmas Lyrics 273
GRATEFUL ACKNOWLEDGMENTS 275
BIBLIOGRAPHY 277
RESOURCES BY DELANO PALMER 283
ABOUT THE AUTHOR 285

INTRODUCTION

Caribbean Theology and Lukan Historiography

This commentary pursues the thesis that the Lukan concept of Bio-Narratives[1] as a way of attempting to write a piece of history could serve as a useful tool to aid in the repositioning and rebranding of the project of Caribbean Theology. The Gospel of Luke, the longest book in the New Testament, has been long since recognised as the Gospel of the poor, the disenfranchised, and the marginalised —themes which resonate with the theological objectives of Majority World theologians, particularly those from the Caribbean whose forebears were numbered amongst the enslaved.

Although the precise nature of Luke's two-volume work is still being debated, few can question his purpose in producing a Gospel and its sequel as his contribution to the thrust of social re-engineering at a time when slavery was an accepted norm. If as Gordon points out that Luke and "quite a number of biblical texts are autobiographical while ironically pointing beyond the authors through the uniqueness of biblical textual intent . . . [and] read as moments of divine intervention,"[2] the writer of the Third Gospel must have composed his work with the intention and anticipation of the kind of divine intervention that was familiar to him in his reading of the Hebrew Bible *(e.g.* Exodus 1-12).

And if the stories of liberators such as Moses and the Messiah were familiar to him, Luke drew his greatest inspiration from the latter whose exploits he researched diligently and whose manifesto and mission he published confidently. Perhaps if the practitioners of Caribbean Theology follow the Lukan paradigm as one way to express their concern over the ills of the region, further progress may come about. The type of reflection envisaged will also allow said practitioners to highlight the contribution of seminal thinkers like Hyacinth Boothe, Idris Hamid *et. al.* The proposal is not entirely new. What is being attempted here is an effort to ground the proposal in the putative writing strategy of the Third Evangelist.

Luke: Theologian and Historian

What these aforementioned scholars have attempted on a more modest scale was eminently achieved by Luke when he shaped the Jesus tradition handed down to him to meet the needs of a Theophilus, and, subsequently, provided a sequel with a universalising literary format with no less persuasive rhetoric. Luke, of course, has been approached by many with a hermeneutic of suspicion because "one of the curious features of the Third Gospel is that, having been anointed to proclaim good news to the poor (4:18), Jesus is found, repeatedly, frequenting the homes of the wealthy (*e.g.* 5:29; 7:36; 14:1; 19:5). . . .Indeed, one searches Luke's Gospel in vain for any narration of Jesus' preaching good news to *the poor*".[3] Also, the extent to which Luke is seen to be a reliable historian is still hotly debated today.

These perceived weaknesses notwithstanding, we find Luke's historiographical strategy attractive because he wrote not just to theologise and inform but to subvert the worst features of Empire. Accordingly, Dormeyer's[4] recent work locates the Third Gospel among "the genre of Hellenistic biography . . . [and sees Luke making] his composition something of an antibiography, using the biographical form to oppose the claims of the emperor."[5]

Although Caribbean Theology is for the most part postcolonial, its potential as a tool to ensure that the Lukan corpora of the poor and the marginalised permeate every stratum of the society is yet to be fully realised. Like the majority of the peoples making up the region, Luke, we believe, was a Gentile. He also saw quite clearly the power of storytelling (with a focus on *bios*) as a way to effect meaningful cultural change. Writing the only Gentile Gospel treatise then (Luke-Acts) in the First Century, one can discern efforts of excellence in his work.

Minority status can be a motivating factor in this regard. While this may explain the quality of his work, the anxiety to outdo himself could be an explanation for the quantity of his output (cf. the following: of the 7, 947 verses found in the New Testament, the Gospel of John accounts for 1407; Paul's epistles, 2032; and Luke-Acts, 2157, over 25 percent of the New Testament).[6] Luke has shown keen interest in Gentile conversions and congregations (Acts 9-28). He also appears to epitomise and illustrate the *dictum* that all our theology must become biography, that is, a lived-experience of faith within community. But, this, to some extent, was an emphasis of the other Evangelists. Where Luke differs from them was to highlight the Messiah's interest in the plight of widows in particular (7:11-17; 18:1-5) and women in general (Luke 7: 36-50; 8: 1-3; 10: 38-42; 13: 10-17; 21: 1-4).

There are two other Lukan emphases that we need to examine. In the Third Gospel, one finds quite a number of references to prayer. What is very revealing is that a significant number of these references surround the prayer life of the Messianic Figure. This Figure not only prayed regularly; he is also portrayed by the Third Evangelist as one who allowed the Spirit of God to control and guide him, and this is precisely how he becomes an ideal role-model. In the sequel of Lukan Gospel which has come down to us as the Book of Acts, the writer appears eager to show that the early followers of the Messianic Figure not only sought to understand their world, but engaged it by the power of the Messianic Spirit in an effort to introduce other-worldly life transforming values. In other words, the theological relevance in terms of a radical social ethic that some insist should become a part of God-Talk in the region was already a Lukan burden shared with Theophilus and company. The conviction here is that the Lukan plot is no mere narrative, but a story which invites us to share its world, the commitment of its leading characters, and its enthusiasm for life.[7]

The Model of Lukan Historiography

Luke, then, I believe, has paved the way for all who would seek to do theology in their own context by underscoring, first and foremost, the value of *bios* and narrative for such an enterprise, since a "narrative communicates meaning through the mimesis of human life".[8] In fact, he invites us to write a counter-narrative to the prevailing hegemonic spirit that has dominated the lives of Caribbean peoples for centuries. In his first volume, the central figure is, undoubtedly, whom we are calling the Messianic 'I': the embodiment of truth and announcer of the end-of-the-age Jubilee, unprecedented and unparalleled (Lk. 4). In Luke's second volume, though the Messianic 'I' is not as noticeable, the influence is even stronger with Paul taking much of the spotlight, demonstrating beyond the shadow of a doubt, the observation that "when God sets people free, He doesn't set them free for their own ends and their own means; it doesn't become self-indulgence, it's a 'giving awayness.'"[9] Now what is proposed here regarding the employment of the Lukan Bio-Narrative genre as one effective way to carry forward the worthwhile enterprise of Caribbean Theology should not be thought of as writing mere eulogies or hagiographies of the ancestors /practitioners of our faith.

What we mean by this is that whatever is written should be realistic enough and faithful enough to the lives that are chosen for scrutiny and paradigmatic value. When Luke, for instance, recorded the strong disagreement between Barnabas and Paul, we see a type of boldness in his literary endeavour that reminds us that theology concerns our lived-experience and the human condition of which we are a part.[10] The creative author of Luke-Acts has recorded for us some of the best lyrics of all time; for instance, Mary's magnificat and the nunc dimitis both found in the Third Gospel.[11] What is not well celebrated—at least in the Caribbean—is the way how Dr Luke has appropriated the songs of Israel in his sequel to his Gospel, in order to enrich the redemptive story he tells. We will look at some of these in due course. For our author, then, singing is at its best when it is the expression of redeemed hearts (Acts 16).

Therefore, the inclusion of Isaiah's most famous Servant Song is certainly not fortuitous. Luke was also well aware of the matriarchs and patriarchs who provided the necessary biblical role-modelling for his day and whose lives were handled in such a way as to highlight certain episodes which would serve as encouragement for people of faith. We have in mind here people like Sarah and Abraham. Fitzmyer for instance, comments on how Paul in Romans 4 "passes over the fact that Abraham was convulsed in laughter at the thought that he might beget a son."[12]

INTRODUCTION

In fact, both Abraham (Gen. 17:17) and Sarah (Gen. 18:12) appear to have gained some measure of comic relief from the promise, and not at their own expense. So both incidents are, to use Fitzmyer's language, "passed over" in what may be called paschal silence. This literary phenomenon is not limited to Paul. We see it, for example, in 2 Chronicles where another man (David) to whom righteousness is credited and eulogised not because he was perfect but because he was justified. Here then, we see 'that historical memory is highly selective and interpretive.'

The popular tradition of Israel, conveniently forgetting the barbarity and disreputable incidents of David's reign, focused upon those elements which appealed to the political and religious aspirations of each succeeding age. John's Gospel (cf. 1:29 with 13:10-11; 17:6) as well as Priscilla's homily (Heb 11:3-40) will employ the same literary strategy. This literary strategy of paschal silence stands out in bold relief against the following backdrop.

The holy books of no other religion depict their followers so negatively as the Bible does the Jews and the Christians. Scripture describes very graphically the doctrine that Jews and Christians are also sinners and capable of the most dreadful sins, and denounces not only the atrocities carried out by the Gentiles, but also those of the supposed (or true) people of God. This pitiless self-criticism is integral to Judaism and Christianity, in contrast to other religions. No other faith criticizes itself so severely as Old Testament Judaism or New Testament Christianity. Scripture exposes the errors of the leaders very clearly, and God often employs outsiders to recall His people to obedience.[13]

One, however, should not overstate the potential of any strategy to effect long and lasting change within a society, within a region. This *caveat* notwithstanding, we are optimistic that what has been suggested allows us to echo, "I have a dream" (Martin Luther King) that a "change is going to come" (Sam Cooke): a change in doing Caribbean theology as a just and justifiable response to regional reality, including the painful experience of dysfunctional family structures, the challenges of violent crime, gender struggle, issues of regional governance and mimicry, poverty, and the like.

---

[1] The literary genre of both Lukan volumes. See Martin Hengel, *The Four Gospel and the One Gospel of Jesus Christ* (Harrisburg, Pennsylvania, 2000), 2.

[2] L Gordon, "The Problem of Biography." *Small Axe* 4 (1998): 49.

[3] J. B. Green, "Good news to whom? Jesus and the Poor in the Gospel of Luke, in *Jesus of Nazareth, Lord and Christ: Essays on the Historical Jesus and New Testament Christology* (Carlisle, UK: Paternoster, 1994), 59. One answer to Dr Green's dilemma comes from Dr David Cheung: "If you want to help the poor, you must disciple the rich. If you want to help the rich, you must understand their poverty." Cited in *Bethel Journal of Christian Theology and Ministry* vol. 2 (February 2012), p. 5.

[4] D. Dormeyer, *The Gospel of Luke*. Stuttgart: KBW, 2011. See review below.

[5] E. Boring, http://www.bookreviews.org/pdf/8360_9143.pdf.

[6] D. Bock, *A Theology of Luke and Acts*. (Grand Rapids: Zondervan, 2012), 27.

INTRODUCTION

7. D V Palmer, 'Lukan Historiography and Caribbean Theology' in Contending Voices in Caribbean Theology, eds. Judith Soares and Oral Thomas (Kingston: Jugaro, 2019), 14.

[8] B. Waltke, *OT Theology* (Grand Rapids: Zondervan, 2007), 93.

[9] J. Edwards, *The Jamaican Diaspora* (Kingston: Morgan Ministries International, 1998), 18.

[10] (Acts 15: 39: Paal an Baanabas kech op [Gk. paroxysmos] an tingz get so bad dat dem kudn sekl it). The same treatment is given to Peter (Acts 10: 14: "Uu mi? No Laad, ou mi fi du dat?).

[11] D L Turner, *Interpreting the Gospels and Acts: An Exegetical Handbook* (Grand Rapids: Kregel, 2019), 49-52.

[12] *Romans* (NY: Anchor, 1993), 387.

[13] T Schirrmacker, *Toward a Theology of Martyrdom* (Bonn: VKW, 2008), 43.

Caribbean Theology and the NT: An Update

Over the years Caribbean theologians have shown more than a passing interest in the NT.[14] If they insist that their starting point for doing theology is their lived-experience in the shadow of Empire, this must never be understood to mean they have devalued the NT as a source and point of departure for theological reflection. For example, Dr Horace Russell expounds both the Lord's Prayer and the Beatitudes from the First Gospel for wider church circles, and a former colleague, Craig Keener, documents the following about his early ministry:

Dr Horace Russell, former president of the United Theological College of the West Indies and for many years one of my senior colleagues at the Palmer Theological Seminary shared with me some of his experiences. He noted that experiences that believers would construe as miracles are common in Jamaica where he began his ministry . . . He noted that they are nevertheless not limited to believers. An agnostic professor at the University of the West Indies in Kingston was dying of cancer; though she did not believe, she allowed him to pray for her. The next day she recovered and has remained well, though she has chosen to remain an agnostic.[15]

Dr Chisholm, former academic dean of the Caribbean Graduate School of Theology, has also done much research on Matthew chapters 5 and 19 on the question of divorce and remarriage. He has also done detailed exegesis

INTRODUCTION

on Matthew 24 regarding the coming of Christ.[16] Wedderburn and Roper have intriguing pieces on Mark 5. The latter compares the biblical account of Legion with certain regional realities. "Caribbean Theology," he insists, "must therefore pursue the triple task of exorcism, iconoclasm and holism through the congregational life and the prophetic witness of the church in the public square."[17] Drs Spencer, Miller, Vassel, González, and David Pearson have sought to provide interesting readings of the Third Gospel by exploring feminist and socio-political concerns.[18]

A worthwhile contribution has also come from former UTCWI president William Watty on the Fourth Gospel along the lines of a creative biographical sketch; John, he observes:

> Makes use of anonymity as a response to a pastoral situation which seems to have necessitated a corrective to a developing Petrine tradition. 'Peter' stands for a negative strain in the gospel. The name focuses and highlights precisely what the evangelist wishes to correct. He goes out of his way to present a 'Peter of history' with warts and all, because, presumably, the name bestowed by Jesus was assuming an inordinate importance. Between the 'Peters' and the 'not Peters' an invidious distinction was being encouraged which augured ill. Names given by Jesus were becoming a stumbling-block, for 'Peter' identified not merely a person but a category of discipleship, a tradition and a generation. Included in that name were the first disciples who were the companions of Jesus and saw the Word made flesh. Their 'names' therefore

created an unhealthy distinction between them and the 'others' who laboured but who were never disciples and therefore could never be 'named.' To correct this unhealthy situation which the mere fact of proximity to Jesus precipitated, names are withheld, even the disciple whom Jesus loved is unnamed and 'Peter' gradually but steadily peters out.

Also making a contribution to the study of John's Gospel is Professor Denise Riley who seeks to demonstrate that the Johannine commission is not only theocentric but Christo- centric to the core, "and is equivalent to the Old Testament Semitic law of delegation." Her work also seeks to show the relevance of the great commission to "the present contemporary age with its emphasis on religious pluralism."[19] Segovia's commentary on the Fourth Gospel fits squarely in the postcolonial tradition.[20]

Regarding Luke's second volume, Roper examined the spread of the Messianic Community in light of the seditious charges brought against it, while Murrell skilfully applies subversive hermeneutical elements to preaching in the region. Jacobs on the other hand did a careful study on the issue of tongues-speaking in the first thirty years of the church. Padilla breaks new ground in his analysis of the speeches of Gamaliel, Gallio, Demetrious, Lysias, Tertullus, and Festus. He concludes that these discourses from 'outsiders' reinforce the special status of the people of God in the First Century through the divine authority exercised over the religio-political milieu.[21]

INTRODUCTION

Recently Linton challenges the traditional reading of the book of Romans which presents humanity as sinners first and foremost instead of focusing attention on the value of the human person. Dennis's contribution begins with an exposition of Romans 12:5, the first one-another passage in the letter. Later he treats verse 10 of the same chapter before looking at several other passages of similar character. He is probably the first Caribbean theologian to incorporate an indigenous translation in his work.[22]

In her reading of the famous NT love chapter Spencer-Miller[23] set herself the following objectives: "to indicate a hermeneutic and methodology for doing Caribbean biblical exegesis and Caribbean theology . . . [and] to arrive at an understanding of 'LOVE' that is both biblical and Caribbean." Her approach which is both descriptive and investigative yields the following chiastic structure:

A Exhortation (1 Cor. 12: 31b)
B Comparison (1 Cor. 13: 1-3)
   C Characteristics (1 Cor. 13: 4-7)
B· Comparison (1 Cor. 13: 8-13)
A· Exhortation (1 Cor. 14: 1a)

A few Caribbean nationals have treated the letter to the Ephesians in one way or the other. We have, for example, Fritzner Dunois's Pauline theology of marriage and Gosnell Yorke's post-colonial exposition, Dameon Black's church growth assessment in light of the ascension and subsequent distribution of gifts, Napoleon Black's similar study from a significantly different angle, Garnett Roper's exposition of chapter 4, and Yorke's post-colonial treatment. Last but by no means least; Winedt published an insightful piece on certain implications regarding the translation of Eph. 6:2 in a Caribbean setting.[24]

Dr Donovan Thomas's series on Philippians in the *Daily Gleaner*[25] has become a model of biblical and public engagement, and Silva has left his mark on the same book[26] which elicits the following comments from the *Expository Times*: "An attractive exegesis of the letter with the minimum of distractions." Earlmont Williams highlights the *missio Dei* (the divine mission) in First Thessalonians,[27] and Thompson, in his massive study of Second Thessalonians, focused his attention on the apocalyptic vision of chapter one.[28] Both Noelliste[29] and Thompson make full use of the Pastoral and Johannine epistles in their concern to highlight the imperative of sound theology. It is Taylor and Thomas[30] who have shed much light upon the situation of Onesimus, especially against the background of Roman imperialism.

Arguably, C. Adrian Thomas has written the best treatise on the warning passages in the book of Hebrews and Maynard-Reid's classic is enjoying a new lease on life.[31] HoSang has championed the cause of Peter's primitive Christian perspective on the inauguration and termination of the New Age as the primary key to interpreting his first epistle, and Joseph its literary structure.[32] In more recent times Baldwin[33] published his dissertation on the textual criticism of the Catholic Epistles. Pastor Teddy Jones' exposition of the Epistles of John is quite sobering to say the least.[34] Taylor's work,[35] part of his doctoral thesis, ex-

INTRODUCTION

plores the significance of the letters to the seven churches in Revelation chapters 2-3 in a pastorally sensitive manner. Williams on the other hand focuses his attention on the "seven heavenly spirits" mentioned in the book,[36] while Dr Garnett Roper grounds his argument for public justice in relation to the Jamaican work-force by citing a most unfortunate characteristic of Empire:

> The New Testament book of Revelation, the 18th chapter, discusses the fall of Babylon. It depicts the collapse of the Roman metropolitan centre which was then the locus imperium. It disguises it by appearing to speak about the ancient city of Babylon. In a telling paragraph, it betrays the reason for the collapse of Babylon that it says 'sank like a millstone to the bottom of the sea'. It puts a lament on the lips of merchants and traders who weep for the loss of markets and trading opportunity and in so doing, lists the products they traded in descending order of importance.
>
> They said: "The merchants of the earth will weep and mourn over her because no one buys their cargo anymore -12 cargos of gold, silver, precious stones and pearls; fine linen, purple, silk and scarlet cloth; every sort of citron wood, and articles of every kind made of ivory, costly wood, bronze, iron and marble; 13 cargoes of cinnamon and spice, of incense, myrrh and frankincense, of wine and olive oil, of fine flour and wheat; cattle and sheep; horses and carriages; and human beings sold as slaves."
>
> In the view of the biblical writer, Babylon sank because people/workers became the least of its priorities. The future of the economy without the worker at its centre and without the improvement of people's quality of life as

its ultimate goal is to hit rock bottom. However spectacular its physical infrastructure and its service efficiency, it will be like an empty lot if people are not the central beneficiary.[37]

Other works provide significant background material for a NTT of the Caribbean.[38]

Methodology

What, then, is the best approach to the study of the book of Acts? First we have to learn as much as possible about the type of literature (*literary genre*) with which we are dealing, for:

A literary genre is like a map, a map made of words. There are different kinds of maps—maps of roads, of geological characteristics, of historical incidents, of the stars—each with its own 'scale', that is, its own peculiar relation to reality. Knowing the scale makes a difference if one is on foot: does an inch equal one mile or one hundred? Establishing a text's genre is perhaps the most important interpretive move one can make. Only when we know what kind of whole we have before us, will we be able to understand the individual parts.

Many misunderstandings of the Bible stem from a failure to appreciate its genre. When this happens, we make a category mistake; we read a text as if it were one thing when actually it is something quite different. Consider the Bible, then, as a collection of verbal maps—a 'word' atlas. Christians plot their location in history not by the stars but

INTRODUCTION

by means of biblical texts. 'You are here'—living between the times, between the first and second coming of Christ, just as Paul was. The Bible tells us not only where we are, but where we should be. We can locate ourselves on a moral map; we can determine whether we are in or out of God's will.[39]

We will also focus attention on the few occurrences of the sometimes theologically pregnant *egō* ("I"),[40] bearing in mind that:

> though all people on planet earth, as far as we can verify, use the word "I" and its equivalents, the meanings invested in that word in the various social systems of the world are often radically different... The way people deal with the self can be plotted on a line whose extreme axes are individualism (awareness of a unique and totally independent "I") on the one hand, and collectivism (awareness of an "I" that has nearly everything in common with the kinship group and its spin-offs.[41]

The pronominal language of Luke, like that of Paul, generally speaking, tends to be self-effacing and quite out of character with the Graeco-Roman world. In fact, in the book of Acts Luke prefers to write about "we" rather than "I". But he does include the I-statements of his friend, Paul, and that of a few others.

This partially explains Luke and Paul's choice of the lifeless and life-eclipsing cross as a symbol of power. In this regard, Paul himself could say with all seriousness: "But God forbid that I should boast except in the cross of our Lord Jesus Christ, by whom the world has been crucified to me, and I to the world;" (Gal. 6:14).

And as to his self-deprecatory statements we read:

"For I am the least of the apostles, who am not worthy to be called an apostle, because I persecuted the church of God" (1 Cor 15:9).

"To me, who am less than the least of all the saints, this grace was given, that I should preach among the Gentiles the unsearchable riches of Christ" (Eph. 3:8).

"This is a faithful saying and worthy of all acceptance, that Christ Jesus came into the world to save sinners, of whom I am chief" (I Tim.1:15).

All this is a part of their weakness[42] language that enables the Pauline circle to communicate to people their own philosophy of life summed up in texts like Luke 19:10, Acts 4:12, 2 Corinthians 12:9 and 1 Cor. 15:10, within their contexts.

Whereas grammarians are uncertain as to whether *egō* is invariably emphatic, a survey of the Lukan and Pauline writings reveals a variety of functions not unlike the prominent pronominal in RastafarI lexicon.[43] First, the pronoun sometimes serves as an autobiographical index (Acts 11; 26). Other times it is used to highlight apostolic authority (Gal 1:12) or to underscore an interpretative situation which may be connected somehow to apostolic authority (Acts 20:25; Gal. 2:19-20). B. Dodd has also ably demonstrated that the Pauline 'I' functions in various contexts in a paradigmatic sense:"In places Paul's self-references engage the pastoral situation faced, while in other places his self-characterizations may have more to do with generally held social requirements surrounding self-discussion. He often uses paradigmatic 'I' expressions as punch lines, summarizing and providing a transition to the next phase of his letters, and at other times his self-exemplification and personal example is at the heart of his argument."[44]

Luke wrote much (especially in Acts 19-20) about a region where the most famous I-statements in the ancient world were uttered: *Vini, Vide, Vici* (I came, I saw, I conquered).[45] The words are attributed to Julius Caesar, who died long before Paul[46] became a Roman citizen and Luke, an ambassador for the Messiah. The words are perhaps better suited on the lips of the Messiah who is *coming again*, still *sees*, still *conquers*, and whose victory cry ("Finished!") was followed by the final I-statement ("I thirst"), before his triumphant resurrection. In his summary of the OT data, Stauffer[47] informs us that the 'I-style' became characteristic "of the self-revealing God of Israel'. This is perhaps best exemplified by . . . Ex. 3:14 (*I am what I am*) and the introductory . . . *I Am YHWH* of the Decalogue (Ex. 20:2ff; cf. Dt. 32:39ff)." According to Stauffer, God is presented as the 'ultimate Subject' in Isaiah 40-45--the first and final Word, the omnipotent Will and exclusive Source of "revealing and reconciling grace [on which] we are totally dependent." Therefore, similar predications of kings or gods are considered arrogant and blasphemous (Ezek. 28).[48] Stauffer continues:

> The NT maintains the belief that God is absolute Subject, but offers few I-declarations on God's part except in quotations, e.g., Is. 45:23 in Rom 14:11,

Deut. 32:35 in Rom 12:19, Ps. 2:7 in Acts 13:33; Heb. 5:5, and Ex. 3:14 in expanded form in Rev. 1:8. . . . The rabbis avoid this style, fighting against the real or apparent pretension of I-sayings in the name of monotheism (cf. Gamaliel's caution in Acts 5:36-37).

It is against this background—the reticence of the Rabbis to use first person pronouns in the singular, the infrequency of the divine 'I' in the NT, and the shared conviction of the NT writers that God is the ultimate Subject—that the dominical 'I' and that of Paul in Acts (and elsewhere) stand out in bold relief.

A Sketch of Luke's Language

The Greek language has enriched English in many ways. The former Greek scholar and principal of Jamaica Bible College (now Regent College of the Caribbean), Ted Edwards, for instance, has sought to show how heavily indebted the lexicon of the Queen's English is to Koine Greek, the language of the marginalized, which, in some cases, supplanted the official tongue (Latin) of the ancient Romans.

The following examples of Greek words that have made their way into the English vocabulary[49] are given by Edwards: *catharsis, asthma, dysentery, dogma, drama, echo, idea, criterion, horizon, basis, character, panacea, angel, paralysis, thorax, rheumatism, autonomy, biology, orthodoxy, energy, therapeutic, mathematics*, just to name a few! My two favourite are names of the greatest man who ever lived: *Alpha and Omega*.

If the language of Jesus was primarily Semitic,[50] Luke's was definitely Greek.[51] His works have come down to us in this language, and that of the best Koine variety. At the time of Luke it was the *lingua franca* of the Mediterranean world, legacy of the great Alexander of Macedonia; and while Jesus must have been fluent in Hebrew and especially Aramaic, Greek must have been known to him as well.[52] Once thought to be a combination of the Classical and Hebrew by some scholars, we have come to realize that the language of Luke (et al.) was indeed the language of the common wo/man. This knowledge has been vouchsafed through the discoveries of the various papyri in Africa.[53]

The Greek language in general has over 3000 years of history, from the sixteenth century BCE to the present. The Koine, the language of the NT, flourished between BCE 300-300 CE. In comparison to the forms which preceded it, the Koine was characterized by simplicity of syntax, form, and vocabulary amenable and useful for merchants, travellers, soldiers and statesmen alike. This is well attested by the thousands of Papyri found in North Africa, preserving "for us the actual life of the day and includ[ing] letters of all sorts . . . contracts, receipts, proclamations, anything, everything."[54]

Accepting the overall contribution of the masses of Greek papyri on our understanding of the NT, Nigel Turner[55] feels however that their value has been overstated to the neglect of other important features, such the influence of the LXX (strong in Acts) and, what the REB calls, the Jewish languages. In other words, not all important terms in the Greek New Testament can be elucidated by invoking the papyri. There are many words that are best understood against a Semitic background, and even where the papyri shed light on some terms, a more complete colouring can be seen from the perspective of the Aramaic or Hebrew. So, with this caveat in mind, there is a wealth of knowledge to be gained by carefully weighing the vocabulary of Luke in the light emanating from the ancient Orient. Writing on "the more or less *popular*" appeal of the NT writers, particularly that of Luke's companion, Deissmann remarks: "St. Paul too can command the terse pithiness of the homely gospel speech, especially in his ethical exhortations as pastor. These take shape naturally in clear-cut *maxims* such as the people themselves use and treasure up."

But even where St. Paul is arguing to himself and takes more to the language of the middle class, even where he is carried away by priestly fervour of the liturgist [cf. Rom 15] and the enthusiasm of the psalmist, his Greek never becomes literary... thickly studded with the rugged, forceful words taken from the popular idiom [like that of Jamaican], it is perhaps the most brilliant example of the artless though not inartistic colloquial prose of a travelled city resident of the Roman Empire, its wonderful flexibility making it just the Greek for use in a mission to all the world."[56] Since Deissmann wrote, not a few studies have demonstrated that both Luke and Paul are much better literary artists than was first imagined.[57]

INTRODUCTION

Bruce adds,

> Whatever truth there may be . . . that Luke was [also] a painter, he certainly was an artist in words. Many will endorse the verdict ... that his Gospel 'is the most beautiful book there is.' How immensely poorer we should be without his description of the herald angels with their *Gloria in excelsis*, the parables of the Good Samaritan and the Prodigal Son, the story of the Emmaus Road!

Bruce continues:

> It is the same artist who in his second book depicts for us in vivid, unforgettable words the scene where Peter stands and knocks at Mary's door, the earthquake at Phillipi, the uproar in the Ephesian theatre, the riot in Jerusalem when Paul was arrested, the appearance of Paul before Agrippa, the storm and shipwreck on the voyage to Rome, the fire of sticks and the viper of Malta. Renan also said of Lk. that it was 'the most literary of the Gospels'. We may extend this judgement to [Acts] and call the combined work the most literary part of the NT. We [consequently] find more really Classical Greek in Luke's writing than anywhere else in the NT....[58]

However, where proniminal "I" is concerned, there does not seem to be any great deal of difference between the *Koine* usage and its classical counterpart. The only possible exceptions to this are to be found in what we are calling the Bio-Narratives (Gospels and Acts), where the influence of Hebraism appears substantial.[59] The few published examples from the papyri seem to support this.[60]

More recent studies of the language of the NT have returned to an emphasis which was that of early Greek grammarians, that is, on the verb.[61] In fact the modern study is enriched by the study of linguistics, particularly the investigation into the nature of the verbal system. Sometime ago two scholars, namely, Fanning[62] and Porter,[63] published revisions of their doctoral theses in the area of aspectual theory. The latter, for instance, defines verbal aspect as *a semantic (meaning) category by which a speaker or writer grammaticalizes (i.e. represents a meaning by choice of a word-form) a perspective on action by selection of a particular tense-form in the verbal system.*[64]

This understanding of aspect, then, links the form of the verb (morphology) with its function. Although the concept of aspect is closely tied to the tense forms, Porter feels strongly that the verbs *qua* verbs have nothing to do with temporal matters. These can only be inferred from the context. For Porter, there are three verbal aspects that were available in Luke's day. This therefore means that in the writing of Acts, for example, one may very well find 1) the aspect complete in which *"the action is conceived of ... as complete and undifferentiated process'* 2), the aspect continuous in which the language depicts an action on progress, or 3) the aspect as complex, in which *'the state of action is conceived of by the language user as reflecting a given ... state of affairs".*[65] Certain verbs, however, particularly "I am" (*eimi*), found regularly on the lips of the Jesus of the Gospels (and a few in Acts), may not carry any aspectual feature whatever, and so as a consequence may have very little exegetical significance.[66] Of course,

INTRODUCTION

an affirmation like "I am carnal" (*ego eimi sarkinos;* Rom 7: 14) will have exegetical significance in their respective contexts that would be determined not by the aspectually challenged linking verb, but perhaps by the prominent nominative and the contextual force of the discourse.[67]

In essential agreement with Porter, at least at the level of definition, is Buist Fanning.[68] His conviction is that "verbal aspect is too dependent on other features of the context for it *alone* [his emphasis] to be determinative in interpretation. However, [aspect] in combination with other features . . . is a significant linguistic element to be weighed in interpreting a number of texts in the NT."[69] Porter would agree with Fanning's distinction between *aktionsart,* an early twentieth-century description of the fundamental function of the verb, and aspect. Whereas aktionsart is said to describe how an action actually occurs, aspect, on the other hand, "involves a way of viewing the action; [it] reflects the subjective conception or portrayal by the speaker; focuses the speaker's representation of the action."[70]

But despite their general agreement on the importance of the subject, Porter and Fanning, it has been observed, have some serious differences in the way they perceive how this promising approach to the study of the Greek verbal system apply to the Pauline and other NT corpora. For instance, Porter believes that the high incidence of present subjunctives in 1 Thessalonians may have been chosen by the writer to express urgency, while Fanning gives a similar emphasis to corresponding aorists. Since aspectology is such a young and complex discipline, and since its serious application to the NT has barely begun, it is definitely too early to determine its full contribution to the understanding of Luke's usage of the language, particularly in the book of Acts. Notwithstanding this reality, the work of Porter or Fanning in *this regard should be consulted for any light it may shed on even familiar passages, along with that of* Caragounis,[71] which provides important checks and correctives.[72]

Another work that is useful in this regard is that of Timothy Brookins, who summarizes the findings as we have outlined them above but has gone beyond the growing consensus by positing the following:

According to this new perspective, Greek verbs grammaticalized not time but rather the semantic values of "aspect" and "space." . . . I accept the emphasis of recent studies that Greek verbs grammaticalize aspect (and in some sense also space). On the basis of the cognitive-linguistic theories of "viewpoint," "mental space," and "conceptual blending," however, I argue that time also remained a grammaticalized, or semantic, feature of indicative verb forms, I [also] demonstrate that particular tense forms correspond invariably with particular times, relative to projected mental space: the imperfect, aorist, perfect, and pluperfect with anterior time; the present with contemporaneous time; and the future with posterior time. In short, Greek indicative verbs grammaticalize aspect as well as time and (in the cases of the perfect and pluperfect) distinctive configurations of mental spaces.[73]

INTRODUCTION

The character of the Greek of Luke (which reminds us so much of the JNT) and the other NT writers may best be summarized in the words of a twentieth-century translator:

I must, in common justice, confess here that for many years I had viewed the Greek of the New Testament with a rather snobbish disdain. I had read the best of Classical Greek both at school and Cambridge for over ten years. To come down to the *Koine* of the first century A.D. seemed, I have sometimes remarked rather uncharitably, like reading Shakespeare for some years and turning to the Vicar's letter in the Parish Magazine! But I think now that I was wrong: I can see that the expression of the Word of God in ordinary workaday language is all a piece with God's incredible humility in becoming Man in Jesus Christ. And, further, the language itself is not as pedestrian as I had at first supposed.[74]

We turn now to some of Luke's pedagogical emphases.

A Sketch of Luke's Theology

Our chief aim in this section is to map out some of the writer's contribution, with the aid of a creedal document[75] framed in the last century.

The Word of God

Many books on Systematic Theology are heavily indebted to Luke's friend for his statement to young Timothy on the trustworthiness of the Hebrew Bible (2 Tim 3:16). The statement outlines the usefulness of Scripture in terms of its doctrinal, practical, and spiritual benefits. The term "inspired" literally means to "breathe out." That is what we do when we speak, and this action provides a suitable image of how God's Word comes to us. Inspiration, then, is the result of God "breathing" out his word to his people. In Acts chapters 2, 7, 13, and 15 (see especially 20:32), Luke demonstrates just how reliant he was on these Scriptures to craft his work, which was also informed as well by the Jesus tradition[76] (e.g., 20:35 and the Third Gospel). In the book of Acts in particular Dr Luke shows how the Word of God proclaimed is the driving force behind the growth and multiplication of the people of God. Pao, for instance, observes that:

> The frequency of the appearance of the term λόγος [*logos*, word] in Acts is itself noteworthy. In Acts the phrase *ho logos theou* [the word of God] appears eleven times, while the phrase *ho logos kuriou* [the word of the Lord] appears ten times. Other phrases that should be considered include ὁ λόγος τῆς σωτηρίας [the word of salvation] (Acts 13:26), τῷ λόγῳ τῆς χάριτος αὐτοῦ [the word of his grace] (14:3; 20;32), and τὸν λόγον τοῦ εὐαγγελίου [the word of the gospel] (15:7). In addition, the absolute use of the term λόγος can be found throughout the first twenty chapters of Acts.[77]

God

In all of Acts the unity, sovereignty,[78] sufficiency, and glory of the Supreme Being are all highlighted (14:15-17;

INTRODUCTION

17:24-25). Acts also (like Luke 3:21; John 14:15-16) laid the groundwork for the understanding of God as a Triune Being[79] (Acts 1:4-5; 20:28; cf. Gal. 4:4-6; I Cor. 8:6; Phil 2:5, 6; Col. 2:9; cf. Matt. 28:19). This is one of the most difficult doctrines to grasp. It is important for the Christian not to reject it because s/he cannot understand it. The doctrine states that there is only *one* Supreme Being whom we call God. This Being uniquely exists in three persons identified in the New Testament as Father, Son, and Holy Spirit (Matt 28:19).[80] Mysteriously, both the Spirit (Rom. 8:26-27) and the Son (Rom. 8:34) are praying for believers. It is the Father who answers the prayers. "The relationship of all three members of the Godhead is harmonious and simultaneous in operations yet in the provision of man's salvation each makes a distinctive contribution. (Eph. 2:18)"[81] The thrust of this statement is to demonstrate the perfect co-operation among the Spirit, Son, and Father as they seek to accomplish especially the divine scheme of redemption. This is beautifully brought out in Eph 1, where the "distinctive contribution" of the Father (vv. 3-7), Son (vv. 7-12), and Spirit (vv.13-14) are itemised and celebrated (*Nota Bene*, "To the praise of His glory;" vv. 6, 12, 14, connected to each Person). A similar passage is I Cor. 12:4-6, where spiritual gifts are in focus.

Jesus the Messiah

In Acts Jesus is presented as Lord (1:6; 10:36) and sole Saviour (4:12). Luke's co-worker, the apostle to the Gentiles evidently believed in the deity of Christ (Rom. 9:5; cf.

Acts 2:21; 20:34).[82] This is of paramount importance. Rejection of this truth means dishonouring the Father (cf. John 5:22-23; Heb1:5-8). He affirmed the full humanity and sinlessness of Christ, who is uniquely divine and human at the same time (Phil. 2:5-8; cf. John 20:28). Scholars call this the theanthropic union. Here an interesting comparison can be made with the doctrine of the Trinity, which states that God is one *being* but three *persons*. In the theanthropic union we have one *person* but two *beings* (human and divine). Paul also affirmed the restorative work of the Messiah relative to Adam's loss.

The fact is that His redemptive work (i.e., Messiah's death and bodily[83] resurrection) accomplished far more than what Adam lost (Eph. 1:3-14; Rom. 5:12-21; Rom. 4:24, 25, 8:34). The chief function of our Lord's priestly office right now appears to be that of advocacy (Rom. 8:34; cf. Heb. 4:14-16; 7:25; I John 2:1). Along with this vital ministry, he is preparing a place for the redeemed (John14:1-4), sanctifying believers (Eph. 5:28-29), distributing spiritual gifts (Eph. 4:7-11), and empowering his people to bear fruit (John 15:1-10).

Holy Spirit

Perhaps the greatest activity in which the Spirit played a significant role was the founding of the Church, the body of Christ (Acts 2; cf. I Cor. 12:13). The Spirit continues to minister to the members of the Messianic community in a number of ways including:

INTRODUCTION

1. *Direction.* He provides divine guidance (Acts 8:29; cf. Rom. 8:13-14)

2. *Empowerment.* He enables believers (Acts 1:6-8; cf. Gal. 5:16; Eph. 5:18)

3. *Worship and Witness.* He provides help in these areas (Acts 2:1-24)

4. *Equipping.* He provides gifts for service (Acts 21:8-9; cf. Rom. 12:1-8; I Cor. 12:7-8)

Angels

Our word "angel" comes from a similar sounding Greek word that means, "messenger." This meaning pretty much sums up the chief function of these creatures. In Acts, there are several references to these created beings (e.g., 8:26; 10:3; 12:7; 27:23; cf. Gal. 1:8; Col. 1:16; Rom. 8:38; 1 Cor. 4:9; 6:3; 1 Tim. 3:16; Eph. 2:2). Although angels are said to be of a "higher rank and possess greater power"[84] than humankind, it was never said that they bear the image of God (cf. the AV and NRSV renditions of Ps. 8:5). In addition, only human beings benefit from God's plan of salvation, not angelic spirits. The spirits that have remained faithful to God are the elect angels of I Tim 5:21. In respect of the "already but not yet" doctrinal tension in the NT, Colossians 2:15 affirms the fact that the forces of darkness (evil spirits)[85] have already been defeated in the first century; but the promise of Romans 16:20 is still awaits fulfilment in the twenty-first.

Humanity

The book of Acts assumes the following tenets spelled out in the rest of the NT: that humans were created by God as special beings composed of spirit/soul and body, uniquely bearing the image of God and in having moral responsibility and accountability (Acts 17:16-34; 1 Cor. 11:7; 15:49; cf. Gen. 1:26; 1 Thess. 5:23). This basically means that every human being resembles God in some sense. The image of God seems to exist in mankind's spiritual (John 4:24), moral (Rom 2:15), social (Gen. 1:27), rational (Isa 1:18), aesthetic (Gen 1:31), creative (Gen. 2:19; 3:7), linguistic (Gen. 3:9, 10, 13), and governmental (Gen. 1:28) endowments. "Originally the creature man (male and female) was without sin, and lived in a perfect spiritual relationship with God, in a perfect physical environment . . . but in course of time the first human pair, Adam and Eve, fell prey to the wiles of the devil and by their disobedience to God, brought condemnation to the human race. (Rom. 3:23; 5:12)."[86] In the Genesis 3 account mankind's condemnation was brought about by (1) human experimentation/rebellion and (2) satanic deception. The enemy's intentions were to:

- Mislead God's crown-creation (v.1)
- Misrepresent God's counsel (vv. 2-4)
- Malign God's character (v. 5; cf. 2 Cor. 11:2-3)

INTRODUCTION

Although we still bear the divine image which gives us our fundamental *dignity*, as children of Adam we also bear the "scar" of his fall. This accounts for our *depravity*. This model of humanity (a creature of dignity and depravity) is vital to bear in mind as we evaluate its achievements in terms of technology and culture (dignity), as well as observe its genocidal and vandalising tendency (depravity). The former renders man saveable, while the latter points up the need for such.

Liberation

It was also Luke's conviction that: "Salvation is God's provision for the redemption of condemned humanity from the awful consequences of sin: past, present and future, through the exercise of personal faith in Christ and His finished work on the Cross (Luke 19:10; Acts 4:12; 8:26-39)."[87] Condemnation or curse is just one of the awful consequences of sin (Gal. 3:10, 13; John 3:18). Others include man's ruin (he is not serving his purpose; 2 Cor. 4:3), blindness (being unable to perceive his purpose; 2 Cor. 4:4), depravity (he is unable to serve his purpose; Eph. 2:1), and slavery (he serves the purpose of another; Eph. 2:2). The liberation that God provides nullifies all the above and, as stated already, embraces the past (salvation from sin's penalty), present (salvation from sin's power), and future (salvation from sin's presence). One of the benefits of salvation is forgiveness, which may be defined as the removal of punitive action (Rom 8:1). Another is Sanctification, a separation unto God. Its goal is Christlikeness (Rom. 8:29-30; I

Cor. 1:30). Cleansing from sin is a means to that end. Sanctification is also progressive, since in it the child of God progresses in holiness. The full co-operation of the believer in this regard is highlighted in 2 Pet 1:3-10 (see also Gal. 5:16-24; Phil. 2:12, 13). This means every effort should be made to live a holy life as Rom 8:12-14 says. The other side of the coin is emphasized in terms of yieldedness and constant submission to the gracious ministry of the Holy Spirit. This is what the Spirit-filled life is all about (Eph. 5:18). This is what it means to "walk in the Spirit" (Gal. 5:16).

Church

Interestingly our English word 'church' comes from a Scottish term *kirk* which in turn is a rough transliteration of the Greek lexeme *kuriakon* (belonging to the Lord). The announcement of this new constitution of the people of God was first made in Matthew 16 and brought into existence in Acts 2, through the baptism of the Spirit (Acts 1:5). The churches (Gal 1:1-2) or Church, according to Paul, is *Corpus Christi*, the body of Christ (I Cor. 12:12-14; Eph 1:22, 23; 2:14-16, 19-22; 3:2-11). "Body" is one of several metaphors used of the Church in the New Testament. It underscores the vitality of God's community of believers with Christ as head. The church therefore is not just a worldwide organisation. It is an organism of global, even universal proportion. Other metaphors of the Church include "bride" (implied in 2 Cor. 11:2; Eph 5:31-32) and "building" (1 Cor. 3:9).

INTRODUCTION

The local expression of the church, many people find, is difficult to define. For example, do we have a church where two or three are gathered in the Lord's name (e.g., Matt 18:20)? Is it possible to have a local church without leadership (Elders, Pastors, and Deacons/Deaconesses? Notice in Acts 14:23 that the various groups of believers were *churches* before the official appointment of elders (who must have served as interim leaders before their ordination.) In light of the above, then, we would suggest that an assembly or local church is a group of believers who meet regularly to do God's will as it is set out in a passage like Acts 2:42. The New Testament suggests that the regularity of meetings should be at least once a week in a permanent location (1 Cor. 1:1, 16:1-2), with a clear focus on the church's objectives in terms of exaltation (worship), edification (welfare), exhibition (works), and evangelisation (witness).

Paul also refers to the two ordinances of the church: baptism and the Lord's Supper. Some have made the distinction between *real* baptism (i.e., incorporation, I Cor. 12:13; cf. Acts 2:38) and *ritual* baptism (immersion; 1 Cor. 1:16-17; Acts 2:41). The former is an integral part of the salvation event, whilst the latter symbolically represents the former. A text which brings together both senses of the word is Acts 1:5, "John, as you know, baptized with water [ritual] but within the next few days you will be baptized with the Spirit [real baptism]."[88] With regard to the Lord's Supper, the early believers evidently broke bread every day (Acts 2:42, 46), but settled later into a pattern of commemorating it on the Lord's Day (1 Cor. 11:20; cf.

Rev. 1:10). The focus, of course, was never on a day but on the Messiah who died and was vivified. Thus, Paul can say: "God forbid that I should glory . . ." (Gal. 6:14); cf. 1 Cor. 5:8, "let us keep the festival . . ." (NIV). Believers need to assess themselves spiritually to effectively and meaningfully partake of the Lord's Supper, Paul says (1 Cor. 11:27-34). Paul also points to a final assessment or judgement at the end of the day. The three main passages which discuss this judgement of believers are Rom 14:10-12; 1 Cor. 3:11-15, and 2 Cor. 5:10. According to 1 Cor. 3:15, some Christians will not be rewarded. However, even these same Christians, apparently, will receive some commendation (1 Cor. 4:5).

Future Events

Acts 3:21 is a powerful reminder of what God has in mind for the universe (cf.17:31). Paul has written a great deal concerning future events in passages like Galatians 5:19-21; 6:15; 1 Thess. 4:13-17 and 1 Cor. 15:51-56. First Corinthians 15, for example, emphasizes the marvellous transformation that the Lord will bring about in the believer's body (cf. Phil 3:20- 21; 1 John 3:2-3).

The fact that all believers will be raptured at this time and every Christian "shall have praise of God" (I Cor. 4:5), underscores once again the amazing grace of our Lord Jesus Christ (2 Cor. 5:10; 1 Cor. 3:13-15, 4:5; Rom 14:10). Another event high on God's agenda, according to Paul, is the judgment of unbelievers. In Romans 2, for instance, the apostle outlines the principles of that judgment.

INTRODUCTION

Structure of Acts

Schnabel is certainly correct when he affirms that "[t]he biographical focus[89] of many passages in Acts suggests that Luke intends his readers to emulate the deeds of . . . Peter, Phillip, Barnabas, James and Paul, and women like Lydia and Priscilla . . . [precisely because Acts is] the story of the life and missionary work of the early church."[90]

Although the lives of the aforementioned individuals are definitely paradigmatic (see e.g., 1 Cor. 11:1; Phil 4:9), the main focus of Acts is still that of God, his exalted Son, and the Spirit of promise—Ultimate Reality ultimately paradigmatic.[91] This commentary proposes that one way to benefit from Luke's Bio-Narrative[92] in terms of his central focus outlined above is to appreciate his rhetorical skill[93] throughout as well as his artistic structuring[94] of the scroll.

A perusal of the *Art of Rhetoric*[95] reveals no discourse on chiasmus, putatively a part of Luke's artistic structuring. Longenecker informs us that Aristotle's Greco-Roman successors were equally silent on the matter.[96] What Longe-necker detected in the arrangement of Luke's second volume is a chain-link composition.

This enables the author to make a significant connection between his content and style. "From that structure emerges a theology intent on bolstering confidence in the God whose power Luke depicts as promoting the inevitable advance of the Christian movement."[97]

Like many before and after him, Longenecker is aware of the important suggestions regarding the structure of Acts and believes that his chain-link proposal may hold the key in this regard. Based on this, Longenecker opts for a four-fold outline that looks like this:

- **Acts 1:1-8:3** —Early Christianity in Jerusalem
- **Acts 8:4-12:25** —Persecution and Consequent Spread (with the transition beginning at 8:1b)
- **Acts 13:1-19:41** —The Spread of Christianity through the Ministry of Paul (with transition beginning at 11:27)
- **Acts 20: 1-28:31**—The Spread of Christianity through Events that Take Paul from Jerusalem to Rome (with the transition beginning at 19:21)[98]

The strength of his chain-link proposal appears to be its explanatory power to solve crucial exegetical problems by showing how Luke makes certain literary transitions smoothly through the employment of a fairly well known (?) rhetorical device. The proposal is also detailed, covering the entire book.

A weakness, it seems, is that it has no centre, or perhaps better stated, it ignores what is considered by many the fifteenth chapter by lumping it with his "third macro-text unit".[99] I hope to demonstrate that by placing a centre in the midst of Longenecker's outline—better—by making good use of Luke's employment of chiasmus with its discernible central focus, we may be better able to grasp an important element of the Lukan plot. The author's chiasmus[100] also may enable the reader to see four ways in which the willing Deity reached out to peoples of the first-

INTRODUCTION

century to ensure human flourishing for his own glory.[101] So the reader of Acts is not surprised in hearing that the book:

> Exhibits careful attention to structure at several levels... Structural organization is apparent also in units of different sizes, such as the cycles of persecution in chap. 3-7, and individual units such as 19:1-7. Ring composition (chiasmus) and inclusion are means of presenting rounded sections. Chapters 13-14, for example, are framed by a complex inclusion. When travel is involved, the pattern follows the time honoured "there and back" formula, as in Jerusalem-Samaria-Jerusalem (8:14-28). This pattern continues with Paul, who repeatedly returns to Jerusalem, but is decisively broken off in chaps. 27-28.[102]

We will now re-examine Luke's second volume in light of a new structure.[103] Our proposal underlines the way in which the gospel is extended to unbelievers and embraced by them and the people of God in an in/voluntary manner.

A. *Plan*: Messianic Community[104] Go Willingly[105] (Acts 1:8).

B. *Persecution:* The Messianic Community Goes Unwillingly? (Acts 8:1-4)

C. *Protestation*: The Messianic Covenanters Come together Willingly to Discuss the Cruciality of Canonical Soteriology for the Purpose of Mission (Acts 15:1-33).[106]

B.' *Portent*: Messianic Communicators Welcome the Unwilling[107] (Acts 16:25-31).
A.' *Providence*: Messianic Communicator Welcomes the Willing (Acts 28:30-31).

It also enables one to see more clearly the tension and dynamic of human responsibility and divine sovereignty in a different light by accenting the willingness of God in Lukan soteriology (cf. 2 Peter 3:9; Isa 18:19). Finally, it foregrounds the Messianic law as an integral component for theological reflection relative to Christian mission. Although we will follow the traditional chapter divisions in the commentary, the above structure must also be borne in mind.

---

[14] Theresa Lowe-Ching, "Method in Caribbean Theology," In *Caribbean Theology*, ed. H. Gregory. Kingston: UWI, 1995; John Holder, "Is This the Word of the Lord? In Search of a Biblical Theology and Hermeneutics." In *Religion, Culture and Tradition in the Caribbean*. Edited by Hemchand Gossai and Nathaniel Samuel Murrell. New York: St. Martin's Press, 2000.

[15] C. Keener, *Miracles* (Grand Rapids: Baker, 2011), 352.

[3] Russell, *Ten Reasons for Living: Studies in the Lord's Prayer* (CreateSpace, 2011), and *8 Pathways to Happiness* (CreateSpace, 2012); Clinton Chisholm, *"Signs of the End: Rereading Matthew 24,"* http://thechisholmsource.com, 2011. See also Dave Gosse, "Examining the Promulgation and Impact of the Great Commission, 1492-1970: An Historical Analysis," in *Teaching all Nations: Interrogating the Matthean Great Commission*, edited by Mitzi J. Smith and Jayachitra Latitha. Minneapolis: Augsburg Fortress, 2014.

INTRODUCTION

[16] Clinton Chisholm, "Signs of the End: Rereading Matthew 24," http://thechisholmsource.com, 2011.

[17] Garnett Roper, "Caribbean Theology as Public Theology," PhD thesis, Exeter University, 2011, *139-178;* Taneika Diana Wedderburn, "So, What Went into the Pigs?": A Comparison of the Grammatico-historical and Socio-literary Hermeneutical Approaches to Understanding 'Legion' in Mark 5:1-20," CGST thesis, 2017.

[18] Samuel Vassel "Socio-Political Concerns of the Gospel of Luke," MA thesis, Wheaton Graduate School, 1982; Justo L. González, *Luke* (Louisville: Westminster John Knox, 2010); David Pearson, "Luke 5:17-26 and the Jamaican Church," in *A Kairos Moment in Caribbean Theology*, ed. G. Lincoln Roper and J. Richard Middleton (Eugene, OR: Wipf & Stock, 2013).

[19] The Apostolic 'Send'—A Contemporary Issue: John 20: 19-23 (Ann Arbor, UMI: ProQuest, 2001),

[20] William Watty, "The Significance of Anonymity in the Fourth Gospel," *Expository Times* 90 (1979), 209-212; Fernando F. Segovia, "John," in *A Postcolonial Commentary on the NT Writings* (London: T & T Clarke, 2007), 156-193.

[21] R. Jacobs, "A Hermeneutical Study of Speaking in Tongues in the Book of Acts," MA thesis, CGST, 2000; *Garnett Roper, "The Charge of Sedition and the Spread of the Church in Acts,"* MA thesis, Westminster Theological Seminary, 1986; N. Samuel Murrell, "*Hermeneutics as Interpretation: Contextual Truths in Subversion Preaching CJET 3(1999):* 48-67; Osvaldo Padilla, The Speeches of Outsiders in Acts: Poetics, Theology and Historiography (NY: Cambridge, 2011).

[22] Faith Linton, What the Preacher Forgot to Tell Me (Ontario: Bay Ridge, 2009); *Carlton A. Dennis, Mi an Yu as di Choch (Kingston: SRI, 2008).*

[23] Althea Spencer-Miller, "*Agape*: A Two-edged Sword, At Least?" *CJRS* 20: (1999), 57-59.

[24] Fritzner Dunois, "The Ephesian *Haustafel*." MA Thesis, CGST, 1998; Gosnell L. O. R. Yorke, "Hearing the Politics of Peace in Ephesians: A Proposal from an African Postcolonial Perspective," *Journal*

for the Study of the NT 30: (2007), 113-127; Dameon Black, "Pastoral Ministry and Church Growth in Light of the Ephesian Paradigm for Growth: A Study of Ephesians 4:11-16 with Application to the Associated Gospel Assemblies," M. A. thesis, CGST, 2002; N. Black, *When He Ascended* (Kingston: Yanique, 2006); Garnett Roper, "Equipping the Saints for Ministry," in The David Jellyman Lectures (Kingston: JBU, 1999), *Marlon Winedt, "'Honour Your Father and Mother' or 'Honour Your Mother and Father'?: A Case Study in Creole Bible Translation," The Bible Translator 58: (2004) 57-64.*

[25] E.g. http://jamaica-gleaner.com/gleaner/20000729/relig/relig5.html.

[26] *Moises Silva, Philippians (*Grand Rapids: Baker, *2005).*

[27] Earlmont Williams, "The Missionary Message of First Thessalonians" *CJET* 7: (2003) 22-40.

[28] Glen Thompson, "The Eschatological significance of 2 Thessalonians 1:3-12." MA thesis, CGST.

[29] Idem, *The Roots of Deception* (Kingston: SRI, 2003); Dieumeme Noelliste, "The Importance of Sound Doctrine," *Binah* 1(1996), 1-7.

[30] B. Taylor, "Onesimus: The Voiceless Initiator of the Liberating Process," In *Caribbean Theology: Preparing for the Challenges Ahead*, ed. H. Gregory (Kingston: Canoe, 1995), 17-24; Oral Thomas, *Biblical Resistance Hermeneutics within a Caribbean Context* (London: Equinox,2010).

[31] A Case for Mixed-Audience with Reference to the Warning Passages in the Book of Hebrews. New York: Peter Lang, 2008; P. U. Maynard-Reid, Poverty and Wealth in James (Eugene, OR: Wipf & Stock, 2005).

[32] David HoSang, *"The New Age and the Interpretation of First Peter,"* D. Phil. thesis, *Oxford University, 1988;* Abson Predestin Joseph, A Narratological Reading of 1 Peter (London: T & T Clark, 2012).

[33] Clinton Baldwin, The So-Called Mixed Text: An Examination of the Non-Alexandrian and Non-Byzantine Text-Type in the Catholic Epistles (New York: Peter Lang, 2011). See also is useful Methods of Biblical Interpretation (Mandeville: Lithomedia, 2010).

[34] *Let's Major in the Minors* (Kingston: TLZ, 2019),

INTRODUCTION

³⁵*Burchell Taylor, The Church Taking Sides* (Kingston: Bethel, 1995); idem, "An Examination of the Book of Revelation from a Liberation Theology Perspective," PhD thesis, University of Leeds, 1990.

³⁶ Patrick Williams, *The Seven Spirits of God* (Kingston: Jodami Press, 2006).

³⁷ "No Future without Workers," http://jamaicagleaner.com/gleaner/20130407/focus/focus7.html.

³⁸ E.g., Stephen Russell, "Abraham's Purchase of Ephron's Land in Anthropological Perspective," *Biblical Interpretation* 21 (2013): 153-170; idem. *Images of Egypt in Early Biblical Literature* (Berlin: de Gruyter, 2009). For a review of this, see http://www.bookreviews.org/pdf/8240_9011.pdf.

³⁹ K. J. Vanhoozer, "Mapping Evangelical Theology in a Postmodern World," *Evangelical Review of Theology* 22:1 (1998): 3-27. We have already said that Acts is Bio-Narrative, a genre that focuses attention on divinely chosen role models within the drama of *His-Story*.

⁴⁰ "The standard explanation for ἐγώ, as well as other nominative pronouns, is that it is emphatic: roughly, I (not you, or he, or they). New Testament commentaries usually ignore ἐγώ, and if they mention it, they typically say simply that it is used for emphasis, but without any attempt to analyze the purpose or effect of the emphasis. New Testament grammars generally say little more . . ." Michael Winger, "Paul and ἐγώ: Some Comments on Grammar and Style" *NTS* (2017), 68:23.

⁴¹Malina, "Understanding," 44-45.

⁴²Dawn, 49, correctly observes that 'biblical "weakness" is described not simply in that word, but in all places where the New Testament writers show themselves as operating not out of their own skills, pedigree, background, training, or power, but out of their infirmities and dependency and humility. Frequently, the Scriptures picture the disciple or church with images not of power, but of smallness—or the work of God accomplished in the hiddenness of weakness.'

⁴³ Not until the twentieth-century Rasta movement have we had such a phenomenon in any professedly Christian discourse. Says Clark, "New Religious Movements," 494: "A movement that perhaps makes more use of the Bible than any other . . . is the Rastafarian movement . . . [which] is now to be found in Africa, Europe, and

North and South America. . . . [T]he Bible is used by Rastafarians as a vehicle for the restoration of their dignity and identity as individuals and as a race which was ravaged by slavery." Weiss, "Die Rastafari-Bewegung auf Jamaika," also observes that "*Die römische Zahl I, wie etwa hinter dem Namen von Haile Selassie [formely Ras Tafari], wird wie das Pronomen 'I' gesprochen, ebenso das 'i' am Ende von Rastafari (=RastafarI)*. . . ."/The Roman numeral I at the end of the name Haile Selassie is treated like pronominal "I" in "Rastafari." On this, see Palmer, *Messianic 'I' and Rastafari*, 17–39. Theologians such as McGrath and Moltmann have shown some interest in the Rastafari movement.

[44] Pronominal 'I' is said to be one of the most stable linguistic elements; it is numbered among a "basic list of words which are known to be change-resistant. . . . That is to say, after the lapse of one thousand years any language would be found to have 86 per cent of these words retained without essential change"; Cotterell, 152.

[45] Suetonius, The Twelve Caesars (London: Penguin, 2007), . Now we can say: Venimus, Vidimus, Christus vicit (We came, we saw, the Messiah conquered).

[46] The apostle, according to tradition, was eventually executed by Nero's edict. But, according to F.F. Bruce (*Paul: The Apostle of the Heart Set Free* [Grand Rapids: Eerdmans, 1977], 5), history has vindicated Paul in that today we name our sons after him and our dogs Nero.

[47] *TDNT* 2: 343ff

[48] Commenting on Phil. 2:5-8, E.K. Simpson (*Words Worth Weighing in the Greek New Testament* [London: Tyndale Press, 1946], 22) has this to say about a similar passage: "Surely the apostle is here re-evoking the colossal effigy of Lucifer drawn from Isa xiv under the mask of the Babylonian despot, whose manifesto . . . culminates with the arrogant vaunt: 'I will ascend . . . I will be like the Most High.'"

[49] Ted Edwards, *Greek Without Tears*, 2nd ed. (Eugene, OR: Resource Publication, 2014), 4-5. See also D A Black, *Linguistics for Students of NT Greek* (Grand Rapids: Baker, 1988), 144-169; D Thomas et al., ed. *Prison Epistles: Exegetical Questions/Devotional Expositions* (Kingston: DVP, 2001), 50-52.

[50] According to Hughson Ong ("Language Choice in Ancient Palestine: A Sociolinguistic Study of Jesus' Language

INTRODUCTION

Use Based on Four "I have come" Sayings," [*BAGL* 1: {2012}, 63-101), Jesus used both Aramaic and Greek.

[51] Like he did for the Third Gospel, Luke's "effort to adapt the story of Jesus stylistically to the narrative style of the Holy Scriptures of Israel is guided by an interest in signalling to the reader that the narrated events are nothing other than a continuation of the history of Israel": Michael Wolter, *The Gospel according to Luke*: (Vol. 1 [Luke 1–9:50 Waco, TX: Baylor, 2016], 5).

[52] Richard A Horsley, Archaeology, History and Society in Galilee: The Social Context of Jesus and the Rabbi (Valley Forge, PA: Trinity Press International, 1996), 154-71.

[53] The conclusion is that "Biblical Greek, except where it is translation Greek [like the LXX], was simply the vernacular of daily life." James Hope Moulton, *A Grammar of New Testament Greek, volume 1: Prolegomena* (Edinburgh: T & T Clark. 1908), 5.

[54] A. T.Robertson and W.H.Davis, *New Short Grammar of the Greek NT* (Grand Rapids: Baker, 1977), 12-13.

[55] Nigel Turner, *Christian Words* (Edinburgh: T& T Clark, 1980), vii-xiv. "It is important, therefore, to guard against two opposing errors: not everything which conforms to Semitic idiom is a Semitism, nor is everything which appears somewhere or sometime in Greek genuine Greek" (*BDF*, 4).

[56] Deissmann, *Light*, 63-64.

[57] See for example, Spencer, *Paul's Literary Style*, 10, and Keener, *Acts*,

[58] F F Bruce, Acts, 26.

[59] *BDF*, 4.

[60] *MM*, 180.

[61] Porter *Idioms of the Greek New Testament*, 20.

[62] Fanning, Verbal Aspect.

[63] Porter, *Verbal Aspect*.

[64] Porter, *Idioms*, 21; italics his.

[65] Ibid.,22.

[66] Ibid., 23. Future tense verbs are also aspectually vague.

[67] This, however, is not the view of Campbell, *Verbal Aspect*, 27.

[68] Later (p.1) he seems to cite approvingly those scholars who distinguish the tenses from aspect, which is "concerned rather with

features like duration, progression, completion, repetition, inception, current relevance and their opposites."

[69] Fanning, *Verbal Aspect*, vi.

[70] Ibid., 31.

[71] Caragounis, *Development, 317-336.*

[72] After commenting on a methodological problem that may be responsible for differences between Fanning and Porter, Silva, "Response," advises pastors and exegetes to say very little about aspect.

[73] "A Tense Discussion: Rethinking the Grammaticalization of Time in Greek Indicative Verbs," *JBL* 137, no. 1 (2018): 147. I'm yet to digest the vocabulary drawn from cognitive linguistics and the like, but his examples appear quite convincing. A third reading may help my cause.

[74] Phillips, *Ring of Truth*, 18.

[75] On this, see chapter 7 of *New Testament Theology: Identity and I-deology* (Kingston, JA: EMI, 2019). The influence of Luke's companion on this document is immense.

[76] Bible students also speak of Christ as the living Word. The Bible today is God's written Word, consisting of 66 books, 39 in the OT and 27 in the New. According to one Jewish arrangement of the Old Testament, there are 22 books. This is because certain books were combined, (e.g., Judges and Ruth), to make the number of books correspond to the number of letters in the Hebrew alphabet and when this is added to the number of books in the NT, the new number is the perfect multiple of seven. The other important point is that the Bible is a closed canon. Evidence of this closure may be seen in the Apostle John's solemn warning in Rev 22:18-19.

[77] David Pao, Acts, 147.

[78] Richards, *Godincidences*.

[79] See especially B.K. Taylor on the triune God in Dieumeme Noelliste, and Sung Wook Chung (eds.), *Diverse and Creative Voices: Theological Essays from the Majority World. Eugene*, OR: Pickwick, 2015.

[80] See also John 1:1; 20:28; Heb 1:8; Acts 1:3, 4; Heb 9:14; Is 48:16; I Cor 12: 4-6; 2 Cor 13:14; Prov 30:4; John 14:7, 17. Practical-

INTRODUCTION

ly speaking, we must obey the voice of the Father (Matt 17:5); Son (John 14:15); and Holy Spirit (Rev 2:7).

[81] Anderson, *Statement,* 14.

[82] Contra Eisenbaum, *Paul,* 172-95. For a Rastafari perspective, see Taylor, "Messianic Ideology," 390-411; see also Selassie, *"Building an Enduring Tower."*

[83] The bodily nature of the resurrection (a body characterised by numerical identity, phenomenological materiality, and celestial glory) is here emphasized. The Apostle Paul argues strongly for the importance of this tenet in I Cor 15. Without the resurrection, Christian faith and ministry is empty (vv. 14, 17); Christian servants are blasphemers (v 15); the Christian doctrine of forgiveness is meaningless (v 17); and Christian hope is futile (vv 18 - 19).

[84] Anderson, The Statement of Faith, 21.

[85] These fallen angels are also called demons or unclean spirits. They are very active in the promotion of false teachings (I Tim 4:1).

[86] Keith Anderson, *Statement of Faith,* 3.

[87] Ibid.

[88] "Th[e] revision of McCollough's London School of Theology dissertation [*Ritual Water, Ritual Spirit: An Analysis of the Timing, Mechanism, and Manifestation of Spirit-Reception in Luke-Acts*. Paternoster Biblical Monographs. Milton Keynes: Paternoster, 2017] investigates Luke's understanding of the timing, mechanism, and manifestation of Spirit-reception by using three primary interpretive tools: (1) sequential reading, (2) entity representations (ERs), and (3) narrative focalization. While the first tool proceeds on the assumption that any text "encourages one to access it from beginning to end" (45) so as to formulate an aggregate understanding of its content, McCollough refers to ERs as "the mental constructs developed sequentially through the text as the reader ... accumulates data" (3). As a tool for marking emphasis, the literary phenomenon of focalization represents a writer's attempt to specify what constitutes the ideal reader's proper object of attention in any given passage. "The thing focalized ... becomes imprinted upon the reader's mind, taking its place in ... the reader's ER for some particular topic" (79–80). Hence, sequential reading first begets and then develops a reader's ERs through that reader's attention

to the writer's textual focalization techniques. By applying these and assorted other tools to an array of Spirit reception scenes in the Lukan writings, McCollough aims to articulate how Luke-Acts intra-textually determines its audience's understanding of the relationship between Spirit-reception and Christian initiation. He finds that Luke indicates Spirit-reception (1) *happens at conversion* and [emphasis mine] (2) in conjunction with baptism, prayer, and (if necessary) hand-laying on the part of a gifted individual...' This review was published by RBL 2019 by the Society of Biblical Literature.

[89] We agree with Eve-Marie Becker, *The Birth of Christian History: Memory and Time from Mark to Luke-Acts* (New Haven: Yale University Press, 2017, 17) that the "Gospels and Luke-Acts contribute to an emerging literary memorial culture of Christ-believers", but question her understanding of Luke-Acts as more historiographical than biographical (76). Why not both (i.e., Bio-Narrative)?

[90] Eckhard J. Schnabel, *Acts* (Grand Rapids: Zondervan, 2012), 109. After all, Luke was writing a Bio-Narrative (*diēgēsin* (Luke 1:1).

[91] See Burchell Taylor, "The Self-Revealing God and the Human Predicament," in *Diverse and Creative Voices* (Eugene, OR: Pickwick, 2015), 48-66.

[92] On Bio-Narratives, see D V *Messianic 'I' and Rastafari in NT Dialogue* (Lanham: UPA, 2010), 13n 7.

[93] Drawn primarily from the Greco-Roman milieu?

[94] Influenced by the HB/LXX?

[95] Aristotle, *Art of Rhetoric* (Cambridge, MA.: Harvard University Press, 1926): Glossary: 472-482.

[96] Bruce W. Longenecker, Rhetoric at the Boundaries: The Art and Theology of the New Testament Chain-Link Transition (Waco, Texas, 2005), 9.

[97] Longenecker, *Rhetoric*, 8.

[98] Ibid., 233. If Luke was drawing on Greco-Roman and Semitic structural typologies, which I believe was the case, then the two proposals are not necessarily mutually exclusive.

[99] Ibid. By its very nature, as far as my understanding goes, chain-link structures seldom if ever display centres; whereas chiasms do not have to have centres, they are flexible enough to display such.

INTRODUCTION

¹⁰⁰The device may be defined thus: an "inverted sequence or crossover of parallel words . . . sentence, or larger unit." Richard N. Soulen, *Handbook of Biblical Criticism* (Atlanta: John Knox, 19--), 40. On the following page, Soulen describes N. W. Lund's ground breaking work, *Chiasmus in the New Testament* (Chapel Hill: University of North Carolina, 1942), as "overzealous"; yet it has no proposal for the book of Acts. Chiasmus belongs to an author's surface structure; therefore, as J. P. Louw (*Semantics of New Testament Greek* [Atlanta: Scholars Press, 1982], 77) puts it, "This means that if an author wishes to say something (deep structure), he will choose a specific form (surface structure) in which to say it."

¹⁰¹ On page 176 (*Rhetoric*), Longenecker also discusses a chiastic proposal by W. Schmithals, which he rejects. Richard Pervo (*Acts: A Commentary* [Minneapolis: Fortress, 2008], 20), in his useful discussion on the Lukan structure, mentions chiasmus without any elaboration.

¹⁰² Richard I. Pervo, *Acts*, 20; Luke Timothy Johnson (*The Writings of the New Testament: An Interpretation*, Revised Edition [Minneapolis: Fortress, 1999], 220) adds the following: "[E]vents in Acts clearly parallel those of the Gospel. . . The cyclical patterns in Luke-Acts are placed within a story that is essentially and intentionally linear." It seems clear then that the writer drew on OT (LXX?) patterns and techniques; cf. W. G. E. Watson, *Classical Hebrew Poetry: A Guide to its Techniques*. Sheffield: JSOT, 1986.

¹⁰³Divine plan 'A' and 'B': A-chapter 1; B-chapter 8; B'-chapter 16; A'-chapter 28.

According to C.K. Lehmann (*Biblical Theology, vol. 2: New Testament* [Scottsdale, Pennsylvania: Herald, 1974], 255), "Not until the incident of Ananias and Sapphira did Luke introduce the word church (Acts 5:11)."

This is the intention of the command, i.e., willing obedience, e.g., 9:19-22; 13:1-3.

"It is not by chance that the Apostolic Council occupies the middle of the book" (Hans Conzelmann, *Acts of the Apostles* [Philadelphia: Fortress, 1987], 115). We concur. Fitzmyer (*The Acts of the Apostles* [New York: Doubleday, 1998], 538) supports the centrality of the pericope by pointing out that both the sections that precede and succeed chapter 15 have approximately 1,200 words.

Cf. Acts 17:16-24.

CHAPTER 1

1 —**'THEOPHILUS' APPEARS HERE** and in the Gospel. Not much is known of him. The two books in which he is mentioned are the longest within the New Testament (NT) canon, with the Third Gospel bearing the name of its author and being the longer of the two. The *fus buk* (JNT) or as the NIV translates it, "my former book," refers to the Gospel of Luke. Traditionally, Luke's Gospel is closely associated with Matthew and Mark (all three are known as the Synoptic Gospels) because of their striking similarities. Interestingly the canonical arrangement of the Gospels appears to have a chiastic shape with the two apostolic writers flanking the two apostolic associates:

A Matthew
B Mark
B^1 Luke
A^1 John

Their theological emphases may be outlined as follows:

CHAPTER 1

- **Matthew**: The revelatory discourse of the Sovereign (Incarnate Royalty).

- **Mark**: The revelatory discourse of the Servant (Incarnate Ministry).

- **Luke:** The revelatory discourse of the Son (Ideal Humanity).

- **John**: The revelatory discourse of the Shekinah[108] (Incarnate Deity).

The book of Acts then[109] gives us a dramatic account of how the Ideal Human Being, now glorified, went about creating the new humanity (2 Cor. 5:17; Gal. 6:15; Ephesians 2:14-22).

2-4 These verses complete the thought expressed in verse 1.[110] They (like verses 5-12) draw attention to the last days of Jesus on earth; particularly they highlight the ascension, Messianic unction and injunctions, as well as select missionaries (a missionary is a person who gives a positive response to the great commission). Verse 3 in particular ends with a focus on the kingdom of God[111] that was inaugurated with the ministry of the Lamb (John 1:29), and will be consummated with the magisterial role of the Lion (Rev. 5). Verse 4[112] re-introduces the promise of Luke 24:49. It also informs us (along with 10:41; Luke 24:42-43; John 21?) that Jesus ate in the presence of his disciples (NIV). The term used for eating in v. 4 (*sunalizō*)[113] is pregnant, especially against the following background: just about everything we partake of has to die so that we may live and not starve to death. An exception is salt (a mineral). So "Christ is the 'staple' of all spiritual life, and he achieves this by his death." (John 6:51)[114] Given the thought of John 12:24—an agricultural metaphor pointing to the necessity of our Lord's dying and rising—could it be that the narrator of Acts deliberately chose this rare word to underscore the never-ending fellowship between the risen Lord and his people?[115]

> **5-7** For John baptized with water, but you will be baptized with the Holy Spirit not many days from now." So when they had gathered together, they began to ask him, Lord, is this the time when you are restoring the kingdom to Israel?" He told them, "you are not permitted to know the times or periods that the Father has set by his own authority (NET)

The baptism of the Spirit is first mentioned in Matthew 3:11 on the lips of John the Baptizer. It appears in Mark, Luke, and John in slightly different forms. In each case the Greek *baptizō* is transliterated as in Acts 1:5. Verse 5 can also be rendered thus: "For John immersed [people] in water, but you[116] will be identified with the Holy Spirit not many days from now." The *"not many days"* is about ten.[117]

During the forty days of meeting with his disciples the risen Lord spoke about the kingdom of God (v. 3). Now they want to know about the status of that kingdom in light of the resurrection. Given their keen interest in this topic, the apostles must have been somewhat disappointed with his initial response (vv 6-7). But better things await them—as well as the world to which they were called to bless.

Verse 8 introduces the programme of blessing: "But you shall receive power when the Holy Spirit has come upon you; and you shall be witnesses to Me in Jerusalem, and in all Judea and Samaria, and to the end of the earth." The form of the imperative ("you shall be witnesses to Me"), I think, should be carefully noted.[118] It is the same form of that found in Deuteronomy, and there is a possibility that Luke wants his hearer (Theophilus and any other 'lover of God') to make the link; only the love of God can truly motivate the people of God to carry out this mandate (cf. Luke 10:25-37 that segues into the Good Samaritan story, and is preceded by the mission of the 70, too, and its sequel [17-24]). The mission of Luke 10 is definitely a localized one, but the one in Acts 1:8 is global in scope.[119]

Any discussion of the purpose of Acts must factor this in. And however we understand the baptism of the Spirit (1:5-8 vis-à-vis Acts 2:1-3, 38 [?]; and chapters 10 and 11), what is unmistakeable is that the boldness and empowerment for the mission is tied to it. This is ably demonstrated by Luke's catalogue of power-encounters throughout.[120] If chapter 1 verse 8 mandates witnessing, then the first act of witnessing is to be seen in chapter 2 which we will examine later. Acts 1:8 is an integral part of the so-called Great Commission which envisions Christ's disciples witnessing to the ends of the earth. According to Peter Ben-Smit:

the expression 'to the end of the earth'..., while not referring to one specific geographical location, as has often been argued in contemporary scholarship on Acts, is best understood as a way of (re)ordering the world geographically and, therefore, ideologically. Drawing on Greco-Roman geographical and literary conventions, the author of Acts invites the work's readers to look at the world in a new way, with Jerusalem and the gospel emanating from it as its centre – and the rest, including Rome, as its ideological (and therefore geographical) periphery. In this way, Acts proceeds to renegotiate the 'world-view' of its readers in an intercultural and subversive way.[121]

That Luke intended "to renegotiate the 'world-view' of [his] readers in an intercultural and subversive way" cannot be doubted; this is the intention of the Messianic mandate or commission rightly understood. The Commission emphasizes the activity of evangelization—the church being commissioned to proclaim the facts of the death, burial and resurrection of God's anointed (1 Cor. 15:1–3). This Commission does not appear in only one of the Gospels but in all four. In John's account we have the Lord saying to the disciples, "if you forgive anyone his sins, they are forgiven; if you do not forgive them, they are not forgiven" (John 20:23 NIV).

Concerning this verse, Reinecker states, "The Church, not the apostles, is now the authority to declare that ... sins are forgiven ... sins are retained."[122] This is true because the two appearances of the word forgiven are in a tense that may indicate prior action. As Ryrie suggests, "Heaven, not the apostles, initiate all . . . while the apostles announce these things."[123] It is the duty of all who preach the Gospel to declare forgiven the sins of those who trust the Saviour. Before this happens, though, repentance and forgiveness must be preached in his name (Luke 24:27).

The same word for "preach" in this passage is used in Mark's account of the Commission; it means to proclaim authoritatively and without apology (Mark 16:15). Mark states clearly the content of such proclamation: the good news itself. Matthew records the outdoor version of the Commission and gives added insight as to what the messianic community should be doing. This account highlights three activities: making disciples, baptizing these disciples, and teaching (Matt. 28:16–20).

What the writer of Acts and the others underscore is that leading a person to the Messiah is not the end; it is just the beginning of our obedience to this mandate. One notices as well Luke's overall understanding of witnessing is not limited to evangelism in its strictest sense as in Acts 8 with the Ethiopian eunuch, but includes works of righteousness, welfare engagements and worship. This kind of vigorous witnessing resulted in trials and persecutions, which culminated in the murder of the first Christian martyr. 9-11 These verses highlight the events of the Messiah's last day on earth, his return to heaven (with a few fortunate family members beholding the incomparable Astro-cosmonaut!)[124], and the angelic announcement of the second advent. The phrase "This same Jesus" suggests that Jesus did not abandon his corporeality at the ascension (cf. Phil 3:20-21; 1 Tim 2:5; 1John 3:1-3), and the question in the first part of verse 11 highly suggests that Christianity is not a spectator religion: there is a time to look up (in prayer, praise and watchfulness) and there is a time to look out and around (cf. 1:8; 2:1-14).

12-14 In his Gospel Luke focuses a great deal of his attention on the theme and practise of prayer, for example, 11:1-13 and 18:1-14, and here in Acts 1:14. It was in this atmosphere of prayer that a replacement of Judas was made (vv 15-26).[125] It is instructive to note that the prayer theme is continued but not the casting of lots. Pentecost marks a brand new era of the Spirit and the interpretation of Scripture that makes the employment of lots superfluous. From now on God's people have much better things to do; thus, the question:

"Why do you stand looking up toward heaven?" That's the question two men robed in white pose to the apostles after Jesus ascends into heaven (Acts 1:11). . . So then, at [the] crucial moments in the life of Jesus—his ascension, resurrection, and transfiguration—what is it that God wants Jesus' followers to know? I actually think it is less about what God wants the apostles to know and more about what God wants them (and us!) to do. In each instance, Jesus' followers seem to have frozen in the past. Staring up into the sky, staring down into the tomb, or offering to build dwellings on the mountaintop so that nobody ever has to leave (Luke 9:33) ... Unlike the secretive tone of the encounter at the transfiguration, the messengers at the empty tomb sent the women to tell all the other disciples about this miracle (Mark 16:7).

CHAPTER 1

Now, on Mount Olivet, Jesus has commissioned his apostles to "be my witnesses in Jerusalem, in all Judea and Samaria, and to the ends of the earth" (Acts 1:8). In both cases, the message that they're asked to carry—the person they're commissioned to witness to—is the very person the Roman government just put to death as a political criminal. It is not only difficult to believe (that Jesus was raised from the dead and ascended into heaven!) but it is a *dangerous* message (that Jesus will come again, perhaps this time to overthrow the Roman government). Given the circumstances, I can understand why Jesus' followers seem often to be found staring into space at key moments in their call to ministry. In the present world, Christianity has become a more politically acceptable religion in most countries. The danger of proclaiming that Jesus has risen from the dead and ascended into heaven has gone away. In some places in our world it may even be safer to proclaim these once dangerous words than their opposite. However, this doesn't mean that *practicing* Christianity has become safe.[126]

---

[108] all the gospels carry these significant themes of sagacity, sonship, servanthood and sovereignty; what is delineated above is what may be considered major motifs in the respective Bio-Narrative.

[109] Immediately after the first verse, it also provides the briefest summary of the Third Gospel—"all that Jesus began to do and to

teach") (NIV). The order is significant (*to do and to teach*), because when all is said and done, there is more said than done.

[110] For a diagrammatical analysis of verses 1-5, see D.S Huffman, *New Testament Greek: Grammar, Syntax, and Diagramming* (Grand Rapids: Kregel, 2012), 104-105.

[111] For an erudite study on this theme, see A.J. Thompson, *Acts*.

[112] Part of the verse switches from indirect speech to direct; the direct speech is completed in the following verse.

[113] Literally, "eating salt with". See the other lexical options, in BAG, 791, LN, 250, GAGNT349, and the notes of NET (https://netbible.org/bible/Acts+1).

[114] D A Carson, *The Gagging of God* (Grand Rapids: Zondervan, 1996), 121.

[115] Jamaican educator Dr Simon Clarke once pointed out at Swallowfield that salt is made up of sodium and chlorine; both are poisonous substances, but as the compound salt (NaCL) it is useful to ingest under the right circumstances. *Together*, we are the salt of the earth until 'thy kingdom come' (Matt 5:13)! Cf. D Whittle, "Missionary Attrition" *CJET* 3 (1999): 68-83. https://biblicalstudies.org.uk/pdf/cjet/03_68.pdf.

[116] *Unu* (JT).

[117] J. Dunn, *Acts* (Grand Rapids: Eerdmans, 2016).

[118] On this C.F.D. Moule (*An Idiom Book of New Testament Greek* [Cambridge: CUP, 1959], 178) notes, "This is a normal Hebrew construction [i.e., commands expressed by the future indicative], and is familiar to readers of the N.T. because of quotations from the LXX such as Luke iv. 8."

[119]Cf. the following from the Psalms of Solomon: "[God] brought someone from *the end of the earth* . . . one who attacked in strength; he declared war against Jerusalem, and her land." *The Old Testament Pseudepigrapha*, vol. 1 (New York: Doubleday, 1983), 659, ed. J.H. Charlesworth. Yorke suggests that the last section of Acts 1:8, to wit, καὶ ἕως ἐσχάτου τῆς γῆς , is primarily a reference not to Rome or even Spain way out West but to Africa, the outermost reaches of the Roman Empire and beyond, way down South, and must, therefore, be taken as a geographical cue and clue as to the direction in which the earliest expansion of the Christian faith was being contemplated as well. "To the Ends of the Earth: An Afro-missiological Take on Acts

CHAPTER 1

1:8": Paper Presented at the 69th General Meeting of SNTS, Szeged, Hungary, Seminar 6 "The Mission and Expansion of Earliest Christianity," Thursday, August 7, 2014; also *CJET* 17 (2018): 1-15.

May be it is best to see, like Padilla (*Acts of the Apostles,* 99), καὶ ἕως ἐσχάτου τῆς γῆς as a proleptic statement pointing to the mission to the Gentiles; Luke's locating Paul, then, in Rome (the centre of Gentile power) supports this interpretation nicely.

[120] On some of these, then and now, see Craig Keener(*Miracles: The Credibility of New Testament Accounts,* 2 vols.[Grand Rapids: Baker, 2011]); on 1:30 he observes, for example: "Luke does not describe miracles in Corinth, [but] Paul reports them as a dramatic and observable part of his ministry there (2 Cor 12:12). Whereas Luke mentions miracles merely in several locations, Paul seems to believe that they occurred virtually whenever he preached (Rom 15:18-19)."

[121] 'Negotiating a New World View in Acts 1.8? A Note on the Expression ἕως ἐσχάτου τῆς γῆς', *NTS* 63 (2017): 1.

[122] Reinecker, *Linguistic Key*, 17.

[123] Ryrie Study Bible.

[124] "Following his resurrection, Jesus literally defied gravity – He left earth. Christians refer to this experience as the ascension of Jesus. Five times New Testament writers employ the Greek term *analambano* (to take up) of Jesus' ascension. Each time the verb is in the passive voice, He "was taken up." The passive voice represents the subject of the verb as being acted upon. Thus, in this instance, indicating that the taking up was empowered from above." David Corbin, *Monday Morning Minister*, April 9, 2018.

[125] The pastor of a church decides that God is calling the church to a new vision of what it is to be and do. So at the elders meeting, he presents the new vision with as much energy, conviction and passion as he can muster. When he had finished and sat down, the senior elder called for a vote. All 12 elders voted against the new vision, with only the clergyman voting for it. "Well, pastor, it looks like you will have to think again," says the senior elder. "Would you like to close the meeting in prayer?" So the priest stands up, raises his hand to heaven, and prays, "LOOOOOOORD!...will you not show these people that this is not MY vision but it is YOUR vision!" At that moment, the clouds darken, the thunder rolls, and a streak of lightning bursts

through the window and strikes in two the table at which they are sitting, throwing the pastor and all the elders to the ground. After a moment's silence, as they all get up and dust themselves off, the senior elder speaks again. "Well, that's twelve votes to two then." Author unknown

[126] Amy Allen, "Don't Just Stand There!—Acts 1:1-11" https://politicaltheology.com/dont-just-stand-there-acts-11-11/.

CHAPTER 2

1-13 CHAPTER TWO INTRODUCES that for which the disciples of chapter 1:13-14[127] were waiting over a ten-day period—the day of Pentecost ('fiftieth'). When African Jews made the first translation (the Septuagint/LXX) of the entire Hebrew Bible in and around the third century BC, the Feast of Weeks was first associated with the term Pentecost and its cognates. If the Feast of Weeks or Pentecost "celebrated the end of the grain harvest" [128] prior to this point, the present one (v 1) anticipates and celebrates a harvest of a different sort (v 41). It arrives with three signs: a sound like that of a hurricane that filled the house (v 2), tongues of 'fire' on each of the 120 (v 3), and a strange, Spirit-inspired speech in different languages that befuddled the Jewish pilgrims (vv 4-13).[129]

The significance of verse 7-12 in terms of the divine purpose to save the world must not be missed, especially in light of a prior purpose to scatter the inhabitants of the then known world (Gen 11) of Hamites, Shemites, Japethites (Gen 10). A careful study of these Genesis chapters may very well reveal that the topographical notice of Acts 2: 9-11 correlates nicely with the first book of the Bible. Perhaps what is more noteworthy is the way in which 'tongues' ministered to the Diaspora Jews in their respective heart language.[130] If the first significance of the Pentecostal phenomenon is soteriological, that is, to bring all Noah's children under the banner of the gospel of the exalted Christ, the second is ecclesiastical. What is meant here is that Pentecost, through the baptism of the Spirit predicted in chapter 1:5, is the birth of the new people of God, who will later on be called the church. Earlier, Luke's companion in ministry defined the baptism of the Spirit as the work of God whereby regenerated people become members of the body of Christ (1 Cor. 12:13). Many emphasize that the Spirit's baptism is also the source of power for mission (cf. 1:8). Since this baptism takes place only once in a person's experience and that at the very beginning of the Christian life (Rom 8:9), one should look to the continuous/continual infilling or control for power to live and serve the Lord Christ (v. 4; cf. Eph 5:18).

14-21 Notice the Spirit-filled disciples were able to interrupt their 'praise and worship' (1 Cor. 14:29-33) in order to engage in apologetics (v.15; cf. 1 Peter 3:15), followed by Gospel proclamation (vv 16-38). There are approximately twenty-eight speeches in Acts; this constitutes a third of the overall Lukan second-volume discourse.

Two of the major characters, Peter and Paul, are responsible for at least eleven each. We will summarize some of these as we carry out our I-deological probe beginning with this chapter. As we saw above, the chapter opens with Luke's description of an unparalleled and unprecedented celebration of the Day of Pentecost. Verses 1-3, with their strange signs and sound, signal the fulfilment of that which was promised. Tens of thousands of Diaspora Jews heard their own languages spoken flawlessly by Galileans—a group of Palestinian Jews that was least likely to demonstrate such linguistic finesse. But not all were impressed. They were some who were sceptical, even judgemental. It was their misunderstanding, the misunderstanding of the sceptics, which elicited the first apologetic discourse (2:13-15).[131]

Peter's boldness and seemingly well thought out apologetic give clear testimony to the arrival of the mighty Spirit, which is also evidenced by his handling of Scripture, logic of presentation, and strength of conviction.[132] The first OT[133] citation in this programmatic discourse is from the prophet Joel. The quotation functions in the following manner: 1) to show that the Day of the Lord is at hand (14-20); 2) that Jesus is the Lord on whom to call for salvation (21-36); and 3) that calling upon the name of Jesus involves repentance, identification (real baptism) and ritual baptism (37-41).

We have made the distinction between real and ritual baptism because words like apostle, prophet, and baptize (*baptizō*) are actually transliterations[134] and are seldom translated. We further suggest, therefore, that *baptizō* in verse 38 means something like 'be identified with',[135] and in verse 41, immersed. This is in keeping with the first occurrence of the verb in the NT (Matt 3:11—a powerful pun), and everywhere else in the gospels, and finally, in

Acts 1:5, on the lips of John bar Zechariah's cousin. Understood in this way, we are in hearty agreement with Peterson's note, to the effect that verse 38 is theologically normative.[136] But our interest in this speech lies elsewhere; Peter's speech contains the first significant pronominal 'I'. In fact, there are three of them: verses 17, 18,[137] and 19—all from the citation from Joel 2. Verse 17 reads:

> And in the last days it will be,' God says,
> 'that I will pour out[138] my Spirit on all people,
> and your sons and your daughters will prophesy,
> [139]and your young men will see visions,
> and your old men will dream dreams. (NET)

The verse is best understood against the background that mainly leaders were endowed with the Spirit under the previous covenant; and these, for the most part, were men. The "all flesh," is an "all" without distinction—especially gender distinction.

If the priests entered there apprenticeship at age 25 and retired about 35 years later, at which time the Spirit that 'gave them unction to function' was withdrawn, Joel's prophecy[140] concerning the Spirit promises a baptism for young and old in perpetuity (John 14:15-16). Verse 18 (Even on my servants, *both men and women, I will pour out my spirit in those days, and they will* prophesy (NET) basically repeats the thought of the previous verse, with the significant addition of the beneficiaries (male and female) of the gift of the Spirit being called slaves of the Lord (cf. Phil 2:5-9; Moses et al.).

CHAPTER 2

The following verses[141] (19-20) read:

> And I will perform wonders in the sky above
> and miraculous signs on the earth below,
> blood and fire and clouds of smoke.
> The sun will be changed to darkness
> and the moon to blood before the great and
> glorious day of the Lord comes. (NET)

Verses 19 and 20 are couched in apocalyptic language, and the initial verb ("*I will show*" NIV) underscores the divine authority that stands behind the prediction. Everything seems to point to the dawning of a new day—the day of the Lord—a day of divine revelation, judgement and salvation (v.21: Whoever shall call upon the name of the Lord will be delivered/*An hevribadi we kaal pan di niem a Jehovah*[142] *gweehn get siev* JNT). Peter's sermon has two more citations, both from the Psalms. Having reminded the celebrants of the salvific promise from the book of Joel, he then, in verses 22-24, introduces a Christocentric focus with an emphasis on the ministry, death and resurrection of Jesus. He finds justification for the latter in Psalm 16: "For David," Peter affirms, "speaks about him in this manner:"

> I see the Jehovah all the time in front of me. Because I am at his side I shall not be shaken; as a result, my entire being is full of joy, and my physical structure will rest in hope, because you will not abandon my soul in Hades nor permit your holy one to experience corruption. Having

made known to me the paths of life, you will further overwhelm me with joy in your presence (DVP).

Verse 25b begins with an important I-statement[143] (I see Jehovah/*Proorōmen ton kurion*[144]). Conceptually, it is loosely linked to the first word or commandment of Deut. 5:7 which prohibits idolatry ("no other gods before/beside me"). In a positive way, David affirms his commitment to Yahweh, knowing full well that only this posture guarantees stability. The above citation from Psalm 16 is then applied to the First Century Messiah (vv 29-32). Under divine inspiration Peter continues to drive home the point that the resurrection of the crucified Jesus is the basis of his subsequent exaltation and outpouring of the Spirit—the very phenomenon that makes this Pentecost unprecedented (33-36).

37-38 "Having heard this," Luke informs us, "they came under deep conviction"[145] and said to Peter and the rest of the apostles, "men, brothers what should we do?" (v 37). We translate verse 38 this way: "Peter responded, 'Each of you repent and be identified with the name of Jesus Christ for the forgiveness of your sins, and all of you will receive the gift of the Holy Spirit,' According to one authority:[146]

There is debate over the meaning of εἰς [eis] in the prepositional phrase εἰς ἄφεσιν τῶν ἁμαρτιῶν ὑμῶν (…"for/because of/with reference to the forgiveness of your sins"). Although a causal sense has been argued, it is difficult to maintain here. . . . [There are] at least four other ways of dealing with the passage:

CHAPTER 2

(1) The baptism referred to here is physical only, and εἰς has the meaning of "for" or "unto." Such a view suggests that salvation is based on works – an idea that runs counter to the theology of Acts, namely: (a) repentance often precedes baptism (cf. Acts 3:19; 26:20), and (b) salvation is entirely a gift of God, not procured via water baptism (Acts 10:43 [cf. v. 47]; 13:38-39, 48; 15:11; 16:30-31; 20:21; 26:18);

(2) The baptism referred to here is spiritual only. Although such a view fits well with the theology of Acts, it does not fit well with the obvious meaning of "baptism" in Acts – especially in this text (cf. 2:41); (3) The text should be re-punctuated in light of the shift from second person plural to third person singular back to second person plural again.

The idea then would be, "Repent *for/with reference to* your sins, and let each one of you be baptized..." Such a view is an acceptable way of handling εἰς, but its subtlety and awkwardness count against it; (4) Finally, it is possible that to a first-century Jewish audience (as well as to Peter), the idea of baptism might incorporate both the spiritual reality and the physical symbol.

Although (4) is attractive, we have opted for view (2)[147] because, as we already noted, the verb *baptizō* is seldom if ever translated; what we have in most English versions is a rough representation of the Greek letters. The same thing is true (as we have said above) of words like *angel*, *prophet*, and *apostle*, which mean respectively, messenger (spirit or human), divine spokesperson, and missionary or envoy. If we accept that *baptizō* has at least two senses (immersion, the literal meaning, and identification, the figurative[148] understanding), then we need to ask ourselves which sense is intended or yields better sense in contexts like 1 Cor. 10:1-2; 12:13; Mark 10:39; 1 Peter 3:21.

39-42 After the question of verse 37 is definitively answered, Peter provides some final words of encouragement for Jewish progeny and Jews present (vv 39, 40). But what does he mean by "those who are distant"? Is the phrase a reference to diaspora Jews or Gentiles? Possibly both. Verse 41 joyfully informs us of how about 3, 000 people received the Spirit, had their sins forgiven, and were immersed to seal their testimony with the new creation community. This verse, then, is a record of ritual baptism, whereas verse 38 points to the possibility of real baptism. The next verse (42) is a kind of paradigm of the basic types[149] of experience a local church must go through to remain viable as an institution of social transformation and human flourishing (*shalom*). The fear mentioned here is answer to the first request of the Lord's Prayer (Luke 11:2a); where there is reverential respect for God, God's will on earth is done as it is in heaven (43b-47). At this juncture a question arises: If the activities of verse 42 are indeed paradigmatic, what about those delineated in the rest of the chapter?

Verse 43, for example, highlights the miracles of the apostles. Were these miracles the sole prerogative of the leaders, and do these miracles continue today? These are important queries, and none of them can be answered satisfactorily in a brief work like this.[150] A study of church history, however, is very instructive in this matter and

CHAPTER 2

warns us not to rush too quickly in dismissing the possibility of God working through our leaders in similar fashion.

Keener suggests the following chiastic structure for Peter's speech:

  A This one . . . you *crucified* and killed (Acts 2:23)
  B But God *raised* him up . . . (2:24)
  C David says + Psalm 16 quote involving right hand (2:25-28)
  D The patriarch *David died* . . . (2:29)
  E Being therefore a *prophet*, and knowing (2:30)
  F That God has sworn and *oath* to him (2:30)
  G That he would set one of his descendants *on his throne* (2:30)
  H He foresaw and spoke (2:31)
  I Of the *resurrection* (2:31)

        J That he was not abandoned to *Hades* (2:31)
        J' Nor did his flesh see *corruption* (2:31)

  I' This Jesus God *raised up* (2:32)
  H' Of that we are all *witnesses* (2:32)
  G' Being therefore exalted *at the right hand of God* (2:33)
  F' the Holy Spirit (2:33)
  E' and hear (2:33)
  D' For *David* did *not ascend* into the heavens (2:34)
  C' *For he himself* says + Psalm 110 quote involving right hand (2:33-35)
  B' That God has made him *Lord and Christ* (2:36)
  A' This Jesus whom you *crucified* (2:36)[151]

The centre of the structure is JJ', but it is artistry gone awry if the body of Jesus was never buried, as suggested by Martin.[152] In an earlier work[153] Keener also offered the following proposal that encompasses the final verses of the chapter.

A People turning to Christ (through proclamation 2:41)
B Shared worship meals (2:42)

   C Shared possessions (2:44-45)

B' Shared worship meals (2:46)
A' People turning to Christ (through believers' behaviour, 2:47).

The BCB sections are quite stunning, considering the fact that neither the noun nor the verb for love appears in the book.[154]

---

[127] The term "brothers" in 1:14 is better rendered siblings.

[128] According to the *Baker's Evangelical Dictionary of Biblical Theological* (Grand Rapids: Baker, "The Feast **of** Weeks occurred seven full weeks after the wave offering of the First fruits at Passover (Lev 23:15 ; Deut 16:9). It celebrated the end of the grain harvest. Because of the fifty-day interval (in the inclusive method of reckoning), it is also known by the Greek name Pentecost'." ἀριθμήσετε πεντήκοντα [*pentekonta*] ἡμέρας [number *fifty* days ...] Lev 23:16 LXX. See also Appendices 7 and 8.

[129] Some Jewish tradition also connects Pentecost with the giving of the Sinaitic covenant.

[130] Garnett Roper, ACTS 2 (Grace Hour, 15.4. 18, RJR); see https://youtu.be/hYlECJ35Wos?t=29.

CHAPTER 2

Was Paul, Luke's travel companion, aware of this story? His construction of Eph 5:18 seems to suggest such awareness. "Two significant elements are usually identified by narrative critics in assessing a literary work such as Acts: the creative arrangement or plot and the artistic techniques used in presenting the plot." Peterson, *Acts*, 47. These elements are skilfully illustrated, e.g., by the paronomasia of 1:5 and the chiastic structures discussed below.

[134] Louw & Nida, Greek-English Lexicon of the New Testament (NY: UBS, 1988-89), 538.

[135] E. J. Schnabel ('The Language of Baptism,' in *Understanding the Times*, ed. E.J. Köstenberger and R. W. Yarrough ([Wheaton, ILL: Crossway, 2011], 240) translates: "Repent, and *be cleansed* ..."; italics his. The verb is passive. So also Nicholson, *Baptism*.

[136] P. 155 n. 89.

[137] This verse is not in Joel; it was presumably added for emphasis.

[138] Italics added; also in v.19.

[140] For an application of this text to the Caribbean region, see Garnett Roper, *Thus Says the Lord: Responding to the Resurgence of Empire* (Kingston: Jugaro, 2018), 147-151.

[141] καὶ *δώσω* τέρατα ἐν τῷ οὐρανῷ ἄνω καὶ σημεῖα ἐπὶ τῆς γῆς κάτω, αἷμα καὶ πῦρ καὶ ἀτμίδα καπνοῦ· ὁ ἥλιος μεταστραφήσεται εἰς σκότος καὶ ἡ σελήνη εἰς αἷμα πρὶν ἢ ἐλθεῖν ἡμέραν κυρίου τὴν μεγάλην καὶ ἐπιφανῆ. Emphasis mine.

[142] According to F F Bruce (*Acts*, 90), "This is one of several places where words referring to Jehovah in the OT are in the NT applied to Jesus"; and we must not forget that Jesus/Yeshua means Jehovah/Yahweh saves (Matt 1:21).

[143] The other Psalm (110) that is cited in vv 34-35 turns up regularly in the NT. Here it is quoted to lend credence to the exaltation of the crucified Nazarene. The promise to the κυρίῳ (Heb *Adonai*) from David's LORD (Heb *YHWH*) is that the Messiah is to remain enthroned until "I subjugate (θῶ) all your enemies." This and the above I-statements justify Stauffer's (1964) insightful observation that "divine I-declarations in the NT are extremely rare, being limited for the most part to quotations from the OT." Stauffer continues: "The NT maintains the belief that God is absolute Subject, but offers few I-

declarations on God's part except in quotations, e.g., Is. 45:23 in Rom. 14:11, Deut. 32:35 in Rom. 12:19, Ps. 2:7 in Acts 13:33.

[144] Imperfect tense; does it mean, "I habitually kept"?

[145] Gk: κατενύγησαν τὴν καρδίαν. Literally, "Pricked to the heart".

[146] NET notes 84. https://net.bible.org/#!bible/Acts+2:37.

[147] See our comments on vv 5-7 above.

[148] BAG, 131.

[149] The apostles' teaching that heads the list is emphatic by its position; here the Messianic mind is communicated via the messengers of the risen Lord.

[150] For more details, see the following note; a concise treatment is provided in https://biblicalstudies.org.uk/pdf/binah/01_013.pdf.

[151] Keener, *Acts*, 1:864; italics and ellipses are original. Bold type added.

[152] D B Martin, *Biblical Truths* (New Haven/London: Yale, 2017), 211; contra Paul et al.; 1 Cor 15:1-4.

[153] C Keener, *The IVP Bible Background Commentary* (Downers Grove, Ill: IVP, 2014), 325.

[154] Dunn, *Acts* (Grand Rapids: Eerdmans, 2016, ix), believes Luke's second volume is the most exciting book in the NT. Yet *agapan* (love) is nowhere to be found!

CHAPTER 3

THE TWO APOSTLES THAT are featured in this chapter are usually a part of a trio in the Gospels. Christ laid much emphasis on the calling and training of men; he concentrated his efforts in the area of Galilee, which could be considered the 'ghetto/inner-city' of Palestine in those days. A similar emphasis for women was hardly needed, since they routinely came for help (Luke 7:36ff) and readily understood his mission (John 12:1ff). One of the trio was known by the enigmatic phrase, 'the disciple whom Jesus loved.'

Why was this disciple given this special privilege? Was he *that* special? Was it because his family was wealthy? When I first made my probe of these questions, I knew from the outset that there was no partiality on the part of the Master. So why then was John known as the disciple whom Jesus loved?

The answer to this question I found revealing. When John and his brother James first met the Lord, they were nicknamed 'sons of thunder'. The new name was hardly complimentary. It was more descriptive of their fiery and misplaced zeal more than anything else.

In a fairly objective profile of these sons of Zebedee, the gentile Gospel writer, Luke, enlightens our darkness in chapter 9 of his first volume. In verse 46 we are told of a heated discussion among the disciples concerning what may be considered bragging rights. (It is Matthew's gospel that informs us as to what precipitated the quarrel. The boys' mother had come requesting special privileges for her sons. And the other disciples were indignant. Possibly, James and John must have openly supported and defended mom's request.) What exactly Jesus perceived in their hearts we are not told. But whatever it was warranted a mild rebuke (Luke 9:46-48).

What I find intriguing is that it was John who stood to give the vote of thanks in the following verse. Well not quite. Verse 49 appears to present John as making some attempt to redeem himself. After all, *if yu trow stone inna pigpen di fus wan whey bawl out a im get lick!* But John should have kept his mouth shut. Here comes another rebuke in verse 50.

Jesus and his disciples are now on their way to the capital city. Needing visas to pass through central Palestine, messengers were sent to the Samaritan embassy (v. 52). The application was promptly turned down. No surprise here, for Jews have no dealing with Samaritans (today it is the Palestinians!). "And when his disciples James and John saw it, they said, 'Lord, do you want us to command fire to come down from heaven and consume them?'"(v. 54). Sons of thunder indeed!

Needless to say, another rebuke follows (vv 55-56). Personally speaking, If I were Jesus John could never be a part of my apostolic band in training much more to be known as the disciple whom I love dearly! Neither James nor Peter who completed the 'unholy' trinity. All three were from Galilee known in those days for its pugnacious and foul-mouthed citizens.

If Peter's denial of his Master was accompanied with expletives we are not surprised. He was Galilean. If Peter was aiming for the head of Malchus, we are not surprised. He was brought up in Galilee, and can anything good come out of any of its towns (John 1:46)?

So why then was John so privileged? To reach men in general special effort must be made. But to reach really bad men like Peter, James and John special effort must be doubled. Whenever the Lord went on a special mission, he would take three of his students with him (guess which three?) for at least two reasons: 1) it was too much risk to leave them behind, and 2) because his brand of love is tailor-made for sinners (Rom. 5:8). James, a member of the infamous trio, is conspicuously absent from this chapter. Chapter 12 will pick up his story.

1-11 This chapter provides a concrete example of a miracle in the First Century, not unlike the trio featured above. It begins with two of them on their way to the temple. There they met a physically challenged beggar who wanted money but received an unexpected miracle instead!

His response is (and that of those who recognized him) telling (vv 8-10).

12-20 The miracle of Pentecost needed some clarification and interpretation. So is this one in the chapter under review. As in chapter 2, the interpreter is the same and the focus is of necessity biblical and Christocentric. Like at Pentecost Peter pointed out what the miracle is not (v 12), then after a brief historical note concerning the living and true God, he placed in the spotlight the glorification (i.e., the death, resurrection, and exaltation) of Jesus the supreme servant of God whom they had rejected (v 13).

We are further informed that the person rejected is none other than the holy and upright One *par excellence* (v.14); paradoxically, the man they murdered is also the Source of life in the universe (v.15; cf. John 1; Col 1; Heb 1; also, John 14:6), as well as the Resurrection and the Life (John 11). It was this mighty warrior and compassionate king who wrought such a miracle on the basis of faith (v 16).

But what does Peter mean by this I-statement? "Brothers, I know you and your leaders acted in ignorance" (v 17)? Is he now letting them off the hook, or is he saying that they are ignorant of the enormity of their crime? Certainly the latter is in view, as with the case of Acts 2:23. They were also culpably ignorant of the fact that their own Scriptures foretold these events surrounding the Messiah (18).

Such culpability must be repented of and forgiven (v 18), so that they could experience eschatological blessings of gigantic proportions, based on the work of Jesus (v.20)—for "*Heaven must receive him until the time comes for God to restore everything, as he promised long ago through his holy prophets*" (v 21[155]).

22-26 Peter continues to ground his argument about Jesus (vv 22-23) by citing yet another OT passage, this time from Deuteronomy 18:15-19. Other OT witnesses concerning Jesus are to be found in the prophets (v 24). Peter then demonstrates how the covenantal promises have primary application to Jewish people (vv 25-25).

---

[155] The cosmic character of this emancipation is seen especially in Rom 8:18-23, and from a comparison of the old and the new creation: in the former, the Creator started with the material universe before the creation of humanity (Gen 1); in the latter, humanity takes precedence. The comparison also reveals the following chiastic macro-structure: A-Material Universe (Gen 1:1-25), B-Image-bearers (Gen 1:26-31), B´- Image-bearers (2 Cor 5:17), A´- Material Universe (Rev 21-22; cf. 2 Pet 3). Although Luke-Acts began with this larger B´-panel and stops short of A´, the writer was well aware of the cosmic character of liberation— from *Adam*—the first image-bearing son (Luke 3:38) to the *Apokatastasis*—the final immaculate salvation (Acts 3:21).

CHAPTER 4

1-7 THERE IS A BIBLICAL phenomenon that is encapsulated in the dictum 'No good deed goes unpunished'.[156] It is seen as early as Abel's murder, Joseph's enslavement and wrongful incarceration, the life and ministry of the prophets, pre-eminently in the life and ministry of the Messiah (cf. John 16:33!)—and now in that of his servants. Stay tuned.

It will continue until the end of Luke's second volume and unto near the end of the Apocalypse (cf. Rev 6). But such hardship is worth it (v 4). Verses 5-6 set the stage for the disciples high profile trial. The opening question by the prosecutor (v 7) could not have been better (Peter must have muttered to himself: "I'm so glad you asked!")

8-22 Peter then proceeds to explain what really happened on the previous day, and, most importantly, why. Aided by the Spirit, he again draws attention to the power and presence of Christ Jesus the Nazarene—the one they crucified, the One their God resurrected (cf. Rom 6:1-

4)[157]—as the source of the man's *shalom*, his total sense of well-being. In fact, the same Nazarene they rejected (v 11) is the same One in whom their health (*shalom*, their total sense of well-being), and that of the entire world, abides (v 12; cf., John 14:6; 1 Tim 2:5).

This truth did not dawn on the leaders just yet; what was clear to them though is that the dynamic duo did not attend any of their accredited and tertiary institutions of the Rabbinic variety (13). Little did the leaders know that sitting at the feet of Jesus (Luke 10) is the best education ever. Both Dr Luke, who has given us two of the longest books of the NT, and his companion Paul (with at least thirteen letters that are sometimes difficult to comprehend; 2 Pet 3:16) have come to realise this verity.

But how do the leaders get around the problem on their hand? They cannot; so they simply issue a command to the apostles not to go around speaking in the name which is above every name! (vv 14-18; cf Philippians 2). The apostles strongly disagreed (v 20). The authorities could not care less (v 21a). All in all, God is glorified (vv 21b-22).

23-32 After Peter and John are released, they related the story of their trial by the Jewish officials to their own kind. It is noticeable that there is no cursing of the high priests and the elders, no attributing of the miscarriage of justice to Satan and his minions. They instead, together with the rest, drew inspiration from the second Psalm, glorified the God of creation, and rightly perceived that their experience with the authorities is nothing less than lingering animus against the risen Anointed (23- 26).

CHAPTER 4

That this is the understanding of the gathering seems to be confirmed by the application of verses 27-30 to their own context. What is noticeable as well is how their prayer takes for granted the intrigue of human responsibility (of the culpable variety- v 27) and divine sovereignty (v 28). It appears as if they were not only immersed in the Joseph story ("What you meant for evil, God meant for good"), but in the truthfulness of what Luke's companion would later express in his now famous letter to the Romans: God orchestrates all things for good to those who love God (Rom. 8:28).

With this kind of awareness, it comes as no surprise that they pray for a fresh anointing of boldness to continue the good work of human flourishing through the ministry of the word and the wonders of healing and miracle (v 30). The initial answer to their prayer was a mild earthquake and a much more powerful manifestation of the Spirit's control in spreading the word—the very message they were forbidden to share by the religious leaders of the day (v 31).

32-37 According to these verses, the fullness of the Spirit is not limited to preaching and healing alone but to the *thy will be done on earth as it is done in heaven* communal experience as well. In every age there are some disciples who excel in this type of living and giving (vv 36-37).[158]

---

[156] E.g., On April 30, 304 "The last and most punishing anti-Christian edict during Roman Emperor Diocletian's reign is published. The ensuing carnage was so horrific that it was said even the coliseum

lions got tired. The man behind the edict, Augustus Galerius, finally issued an edict of toleration on April 30, 311—just Days before dying of a disease known as 'being eaten with worms.'" https://www.christianitytoday.com/history/today/april-30.html.

[157] Elsewhere the Spirit (Rom 1) and the Son (John 2; 10) are credited with the same act.

[158] The fact that Barnabas is an islander is a great encouragement to some of us; he belonged to a tribe that was particularly known for their receiving: the Levites. He is pre-eminently known for his giving; indeed it is blessed to receive. But it is even better to give (Acts 20).

CHAPTER 5

1-11 AND IN EVERY AGE, there are those among the people of God who prefer to feign the godliness of generosity. Such is the case of Ananias and his wife. Interestingly, the Peter who figures prominently in the trial and judgement of this sad episode so early in the history of the Messianic community also lied. His repentance was spurred by the crowing of a rooster. He will be tempted later on to do the same (Gal 2). The seriousness of lying to God and his Spirit (vv 3 4, 9) is underscored both by the severity of the judgement (vv 5a, 10) and the signal effect on the community (vv 5b, 11).

12-16 These verses, right after the sobering story outlined above, afford us an opportunity to breathe again; they provide us with the fresh air of unity (12), sobriety, and much cause for rejoicing (13-16). But there are dark clouds on the horizon.

17-41 The religious leaders will not give up; they were not invited to the 'party' described in verses 12-16, and so, moved with envy, they once again moved to crash it (17-18). Heaven itself responded to their threat and the good work of gospel proclamation and Messianic instruction was resumed (17-21a).

Meanwhile, the Sanhedrin and company are ready to conduct another judicial hearing but the accused are nowhere to be found—well, the disciples were not where they were supposed to have been, according to the official reckoning (21b-26).

Eventually the re-trial is begun with a probing query (Didn't we demand that you stop teaching in this name? And now you have saturated Jerusalem with your doctrine, and wish to make us culpable of this man's death! 27-28). But Peter and company are equal to the task:

We are duty bound to give heed to God rather than men! The God of our ancestors raised Jesus, whom you murdered by hanging him on the tree[159]; this same one God has promoted to his side as prince and Saviour, in order to make possible for Israel's repentance and forgiveness of sins. We[160] ourselves and the Holy Spirit, whom God gives to the obedient, are witnesses of these matters (29-32).

33-41 In an ideal situation one would expect a very positive response to the solemn words of Peter. On the day of Pentecost that was the type of response the apostles received (2:37-41). On this occasion the Jewish leaders, it would appear, were angry from the very beginning; notice how they refer to Jesus as *this man* (27-28). Luke has a similar report of an angry hombre in his gospel (chapter 15:28-30). Here the leaders are not only enraged; they plot murder (33).

CHAPTER 5

But we must never assume (as some foolishly do) that all Rastas are rascals or that all Germans are like Hitler or that all Sadducees were *sad-u-see*[161] or all Pharisees of the First Century were equally bad. We must never forget that Jesus was buried in the borrowed tomb of Joseph of Aramatheia (a short-term loan if ever there was one!). Gamaliel (34) demonstrates how dangerous our generalisations can be. It was he who saved the day with words of wisdom:

> Men of Israel, consider carefully what you intend to do to these men. Some time ago Theudas appeared, claiming to be somebody, and about four hundred men rallied to him. He was killed, all his followers were dispersed, and it all came to nothing. After him, Judas the Galilean appeared in the days of the census and led a band of people in revolt. He too was killed, and all his followers were scattered. Therefore, in the present case I advise you: Leave these men alone! Let them go! For if their purpose or activity is of human origin, it will fail. But if it is from God, you will not be able to stop these men; you will only find yourselves fighting against God (35-39 NIV).

In the end both the Jewish leaders and the apostles stood their ground: the former continued to prohibit the spread of the gospel, and the latter, as we shall see later, persist in speaking in *the* Name, after their release (40). Verse 41 raises the question as to whether or not the apostles are masochists or mere merry men. They are neither. They are in fact exemplary and proud leaders of the fledgling Messianic community, the church, filled with the

Spirit of joy, unlike the Jewish authorities who allowed envy and jealously to get the better of them. The final verse of this chapter ("Day after day, in the temple courts and from house to house, they never stopped teaching and proclaiming the good news that Jesus is the Messiah." NIV) not only draws our attention to the conviction and determination of the early believers; it also underscores a theme introduced in the second chapter. Another chiastic framework[162] highlights the point:

[A] Temple-house Frame (2.46)
[B] Public-Temple Tour (3.1-4.22)
[C] Private House Interlude (4.23-5.11)
[B'] Public-Temple Tour (5.12-41)
[A'] Temple-house Frame (5.42)

---

[159] Qualitative use of the anarthrous *xylov*?
[160] Emphatic pronoun.
[161] Though one would argue that there's some truth to this, since they did not believe in the resurrection.
[162] F.S. Spencer, Acts, 51.

CHAPTER 6

1-7 SOMETIME LATER, AS the number of disciples kept growing, there was a quarrel between the Greek-speaking Jews and the native Jews. The Greek-speaking Jews claimed that their widows were being neglected in the daily distribution of funds. ²So the twelve apostles called the whole group of believers together and said, "It is not right for us to neglect the preaching of God's word in order to handle finances. ³So then, brothers and sisters, choose seven men among you who are known to be full of the Holy Spirit and wisdom, and we will put them in charge of this matter.

⁴We ourselves, then, will give our full time to prayer and the work of preaching." ⁵The whole group was pleased with the apostles' proposal, so they chose Stephen, a man full of faith and the Holy Spirit, and Philip, Prochorus, Nicanor, Timon, Parmenas, and Nicolaus, a Gentile from Antioch who had earlier been converted to Judaism. ⁶The group presented them to the apostles, who prayed and

placed their hands on them. 7 And so the word of God continued to spread. The number of disciples in Jerusalem grew larger and larger, and a great number of priests accepted the faith. (GNB)

Quarrel in the Messianic community (v 1)? There are times when we so idealize the early church that we forget that they were human beings just like you and me. We will see later the dispute between Barnabas and Paul (chapter 15); the end of Galatians 2 records yet another dispute.

These failings remind us how much we need the fruit of the Spirit to live in community (Gal 5:22-23). Apart from that *dawg nyam wi suppa* (Gal 5:15)! The problem outlined here in verse 1 is that *The Greek-speaking Jews claimed that their widows were being neglected in the daily distribution of funds [and food?].*

The response of the apostles is telling; they knew that 'the good is the enemy of the best,' so instead of getting directly involved themselves by taking over the distribution of benefits, they

> called the whole group of believers together and said, "It is not right for us to neglect the preaching of God's word in order to handle finances. ³So then, brothers and sisters, choose seven men among you who are known to be full of the Holy Spirit and wisdom, and we will put them in charge of this matter. ⁴We ourselves, then, will give our full time to prayer and the work of preaching.

It is important to notice that those who are chosen are not only qualified according to stipulated criteria but ap-

CHAPTER 6

pear to belong to the group with the felt need—to judge by their Hellenistic/Greek names (*Stephen, a man full of faith and the Holy Spirit, and Philip, Prochorus, Nicanor, Timon, Parmenas, and Nicolaus, a Gentile from Antioch who had earlier been converted to Judaism*).

The brilliant—better, the Spirit-filled—counsel of the apostles not only had internal success, but external and lasting impact as well (6-7). These early leaders, steeped in Scripture, must have been guided by the story of Jethro and Moses in Exodus 18.

8-15 If in the previous paragraph we have an account of the first set of church deacons, we will learn from the final paragraph of this chapter that at least one of them is no mere server of tables. Stephen, we are made to understand, was an outstanding wonder-worker, speaker, and, as we shall see in the next chapter, a fine historian and an apologist as well. All these attributes qualified him to become a faithful witness and exemplar for over nineteen centuries.

CHAPTER 7

STEPHEN'S SPEECH, THE LONGEST in the book, now occupies our attention. The structure of the monologue is probably best appreciated by observing its *bio-narratival* outline: Abraham (vv. 2b-8), Joseph (v. 9-16), Moses (vv.17-43), and the [Tabernacle] *Temple* (44-50).

The final section is, of course, non-biographical (44-50), but it appears theologically pregnant in the sense that Stephen's accusers, among other things, spoke about the temple in the previous chapter (6:11-13). The inter-textual links are highly suggestive.

All the evangelists in one way or the other pick up on the key term 'destroy' or its cognate (Mk 11.15-19; Matt .21-12-19; Lk 19. 45-48; Jn. 2.13-22). The last of them, John, informs us that at the time of the declaration not even the disciples understood the destruction of the temple about which their Master spoke. It was only after the resurrection that they finally understood that Jesus was talking about himself.

CHAPTER 7

Stephen's accusers were conveyors of a literalistic tradition which was now brought to bear on Stephen's case. What they and their leaders did not know or refuse to believe is that Jesus is the latest and greatest locus of the divine-human fellowship, replacing the tabernacle (John 1) and temple (John 2). So it is interesting that the biographical focus of Stephen's speech referenced above should end with the *Temple*. A few of the final words of the speech (48-50), in this regard, are also quite allusive. The Jewish leaders, however, did not see it that way (51-54). Stephen's last words (55-56) contain a significant I-statement.

Both Stephen (and Paul later on) saw the glory of Christ, and both were blinded in the process; the former through the process of dying, and the latter on his way to life eternal. Both invoked the name of the Lord. Both were present at the trial (7:58). Like Peter at Pentecost, Stephen, the faithful witness, knew how to expound and apply Scripture in such a way as to bring conviction to his audience, and like Peter (2:14-15), there was also an apologetic element to his discourse.

As Stephen, fully under the Spirit's control, made his way to the portals of heaven, he "saw the Glory of God, that is, Jesus standing" at God's side (v. 55).[163] Then he shouts, "Look . . . I see heaven open and the Son of Man standing at the right hand of God."(NIV).[164] If Boyarin's bold and intriguing thesis is to be accepted that the title Son of God, particularly in the Gospel of Mark, is more associated with the humanity of the Christ and Son of Man His deity, then we can better appreciate Saul's (and that of the executioners) horror in listening to Stephen's final words.[165]

If the fledgling Messianic community was tested internally with the challenge of meeting the needs of their own in chapters 2-4, the lies of two of their own in chapter 5, the imperative of prioritizing in chapter 6, then the test of chapter 7 is overtly external but no less challenging. Chapter 8 (and following) is Luke's report of how this challenge was met.

---

[163]Nigel Turner, *Christian Words* (Edinburgh: T&T Clark, 1980), 187; 'Glory of God' here is possibly a metonym for God himself; cf.McCasland–and 2 Cor 4:6.

[164] Says Beverly Gaventa (*Acts* [Nashville: Abingdon, 2003], 33): "These repeated assertions of Jesus' location have less to do with geography [astronomy?] than with theology; as God was with Jesus (10:38), now Jesus is with God."

[165]Daniel Boyarin, *The Jewish Gospels: The Story of the Jewish Christ* (New York: New Press, 2012), 30-31. Cf. J.E. Taylor, "The Son of Man," *The Bible Translator* 48 (1997): 101-108. We therefore disagree with Barrett (Acts, 383) that "It would be mistaken to lay too much stress on the Christological significance of . . . [Stephen's] vision."

CHAPTER 8

NOW SAUL WAS CONSENTING to his death. At that time a great persecution arose against the church which was at Jerusalem; and they were all scattered throughout the regions of Judea and Samaria, except the apostles. 2 And devout men carried Stephen to his burial, and made great lamentation over him. 3 As for Saul, he made havoc of the church, entering every house, and dragging off men and women, committing them to prison. 4 Therefore those who were scattered went everywhere preaching the word.

1-4 The initial verse of this chapter (1a) introduces us to the first great persecution against the church and—more importantly—the first great preacher to the Gentile world. Saul, later called Paul, is Luke's hero and co-worker in the gospel. To judge from Luke's report, it does appear that the early believers did their best in carrying out the Messianic mandate of Luke 24 and Acts 1:8. But a reading of verse 1b, with its mention of the Jerusalem-Judea-Samaria collocation, seems to suggest that there was still room for improvement.

The first time we see these place names together is in chapter one verse eight. Here the believers are now located in these spaces, courtesy of a severe persecution. We are not sure how long the new people of God experienced their phenomenal growth both in numbers and maturity; one thing seems certain: there was no clear evidence of any plans on their part to reach out to the Judeans or Samaritans, much less to the Cubans and Jamaicans who occupied the utmost part of the globe.

Bruce comments that the "new Ecclesia, like the old, was to have its Diaspora (cf. 1 Pet. I. 1)... The persecution led them to carry out further the terms of their Lord's commission in i. 8."[166] The old Ecclesia was definitely scattered on account of their sin; it is debatable whether their new covenant counterpart suffered a similar fate.[167] If we assume that the church at this juncture was guilty of disobedience, we also note a difference.

The old covenant people were punished for straying (idolatry) in the land, whereas the post-Pentecostal people were guilty of staying too long (inertia?) in the same piece of real estate, particularly the capital where the success was phenomenal.

Did the apostles stick around to consolidate this success, to protect the weak (widows, children, infirmed et al.?), or to make themselves available to answer charges on behalf of the fledgling Messianic community? Luke does not tell us. Luke's interest at this point is to show us how the good news winged its way from Jerusalem to other parts of Palestine (v 4).[168]

CHAPTER 8

5-25 One particular member of the cross-cultural team is singled out for special mention by the writer. This particular missionary found himself in the north proclaiming the good news of Christ to an eager audience. His message was accompanied by signs and wonders, resulting in great rejoicing (5-8).

But as in life in general and the Christian sojourn in particular, a season of blessing is soon followed by a time of severe testing. Verses 9-23 document an example of such a test, followed by another brief episode of triumph (24-25).

> A man named Simon lived there, who for some time had astounded the Samaritans with his magic. He claimed that he was someone great, [10]and everyone in the city, from all classes of society, paid close attention to him. "He is that power of God known as 'The Great Power'," they said. [11]They paid this attention to him because for such a long time he had astonished them with his magic. [12]But when they believed Philip's message about the good news of the Kingdom of God and about Jesus Christ, they were baptized, both men and women.
>
> [13]Simon himself also believed; and after being baptized, he stayed close to Philip and was astounded when he saw the great wonders and miracles that were being performed. 14 The apostles in Jerusalem heard that the people of Samaria had received the word of God, so they sent Peter and John to them. [15]When they arrived, they prayed for the believers that they might receive the Holy Spirit. [16]For the Holy Spirit had not yet come down on any of them; they had only been baptized in the name of the Lord Jesus.

ACTS

¹⁷Then Peter and John placed their hands on them, and they received the Holy Spirit.18¹⁶⁹ Simon saw that the Spirit had been given to the believers when the apostles placed their hands on them. So he offered money to Peter and John, ¹⁹and said, "Give this power to me too, so that anyone I place my hands on will receive the Holy Spirit."20 But Peter answered him, "May you and your money go to hell, for thinking that you can buy God's gift with money!

²¹You have no part or share in our work, because your heart is not right in God's sight. ²²Repent, then, of this evil plan of yours, and pray to the Lord that he will forgive you for thinking such a thing as this. ²³For I see that you are full of bitter envy and are a prisoner of sin."24 Simon said to Peter and John, "Please pray to the Lord for me, so that none of these things you spoke of will happen to me."25 After they had given their testimony and proclaimed the Lord's message, Peter and John went back to Jerusalem. On their way they preached the Good News in many villages of Samaria. (GNB)

The Amazing African

26-40 The mission to Gentiles[170] starts here in chapter 8 with the African,[171] then to the European in chapter 10, and finally to other Gentiles in chapter 11.[172] The mission then receives a new impetus in chapter 13 with the commissioning of Barnabas and Saul and, of course, the divine initiative. The evangelisation of Africans is initiated by a divine messenger who instructed Philip to abandon his successful mass campaign among the Samaritans and head south (26). Did Phillip expect to find another group of people? We don't know. All we are told in verse 27 is that his obedience was prompt, and that his evangelistic ministry is limited to one person—a VIP at that—a leader, a reader, a very serious and open-minded religious inquirer, reading from the fifty-third chapter of the book of Isaiah (28). Rouven Genz, in his doctoral dissertation entitled *Isaiah 53 as the Theological Centre of the Acts: Studies in its Christology and Ecclesiology, in Connection with Acts 8: 26-40*[173], posits that the passage from which the African national was reading is crucial for Luke the narrator. One review[174] summarizes Genz's work as follows:

Part 1 gives us a structural analysis of Philip's encounter with the Ethiopian eunuch (Acts 8:26–40), defining its narrative function in relation to 1:8 and 8:1ff. Behind the apparently accidental encounter of two strangers on the Gaza road lies a convergence of spiritual forces (the angel of the Lord, the Holy Spirit, the scripture itself). The narrative is structured in such a way that the quotation of Isa 53:7–8 falls at the focal point of the encounter.

By citing the text verbatim, Luke invites the reader into the revelatory moment: however, the citation is embedded in a richly textured narrative that evokes a much wider range of prophetic texts, many of them from … Isaiah. Details of time ("about noon") and place point to a significant divine revelation with soteriological import: the wilderness setting (foregrounded in 8:26) creates an intertextual link with Isa 40:3–5, where the wilderness is a place where "all flesh shall see the salvation of our God" (already cited in Luke 3:6). The pilgrimage of the nations to find the wisdom of God in Zion is reversed as the good news of Jesus goes out *from* Zion and meets this gentile as he returns home.

The eunuch is a highly placed court official, an Ethiopian from "the ends of the earth," and a *castratus* who finds a place in the people of the new covenant not by Sabbath keeping or pilgrimage (Isa 56:1–8; Wis 3:14) but by hearing and responding to the good news of Jesus. This pagan sympathizer with Jewish belief plays a similar narrative role to Cornelius in Acts 10 but unlike him is physically prevented from full integration into the people of God. So his baptism represents a significant new moment in salvation history, a fulfillment of Isa 52:15 (MT). So Isa 53 is central to Genz's argument that Acts 8:26–40 is a "key text" in Acts.

Deacon Phillip, if we may call him that, receives further instruction from another divine authority, the one who was sent on the day of Pentecost and of highest rank in heavenly quarters. Phillip's exemplary response is again highlighted. Having joined the Ethiopian in his chariot, Phillip listened carefully to the reading of Scripture in a different accent, and then asked a pertinent question (29-30).

The official replied, "How can I understand unless someone explains it to me?" And he invited Philip to climb up and sit in the carriage with him. [32*]The passage of scripture which he was reading was this:

> 'Like a sheep that is taken to be slaughtered,

like a lamb that makes no sound when its wool is cut off, he did not say a word.

³³ He was humiliated, and justice was denied him. No one will be able to tell about his descendants, because his life on earth has come to an end.'

³⁴ The official asked Philip, "Tell me, of whom is the prophet saying this? Of himself or of someone else?" ³⁵Then Philip began to speak; starting from this passage of scripture, he told him the Good News about Jesus. ³⁶As they travelled down the road, they came to a place where there was some water, and the official said, "Here is some water. What is to keep me from being baptized?"

³⁸ The official ordered the carriage to stop, and both Philip and the official went down into the water, and Philip baptized him. ³⁹When they came up out of the water, the Spirit of the Lord took Philip away. The official did not see him again, but continued on his way, full of joy. (GNB)[175]

Phillip's personal evangelistic endeavour was just as joyous as his efforts in Samaria. "Philip [then] found himself in Azotus; he went on to Caesarea, and on the way, he preached the Good News in every town" (v 40 GNB).

There is more than enough divine joy to go around.

---

[166] F. F. Bruce (*Acts*, 181. He also cites an interesting parallel from 2 Baruch i. 4: "I will scatter this people among the Gentiles, that they may do good to the Gentiles."

[167]Cf. D. von Allman, "The Birth of Theology: Contextualization as the Dynamic Element in the Formation of New Testament Theology," *International Review of Mission* 64 (1975), 39.

[168] Evidently, the disciples were trained to carry out the task of evangelism or quite likely they drew upon their experience of sharing their faith in Jerusalem.

[169] "The Samaritans are said to have believed Philip (not Jesus) in Acts 8:12 and that the adverb *monos* (NIV "simply") in verse 16 must modify "been baptized," not "in the name of the Lord Jesus." Thus, the contrast has to be with another implied verb, not between baptism in Jesus vs. baptism in the Holy Spirit. Perhaps that implied verb was "believed." Perhaps the Samaritans had only been baptized in Jesus; they hadn't actually believed in Jesus (because they had believed in Philip). It is true that the issue is not "believe" followed by a dative direct object, as Dunn had claimed. It is rather that nowhere else in Acts does anyone ever believe (in) a human proclaimer of the gospel message, an observation than surely must also be significant for the narrative critic." C. Blomberg, Denver Seminary. All this seems a bit forced.

[170] The Samaritans were mixed.

[171] Luke begins his triadic show-piece by telling the story of a Gentile treasurer, who may well have been regarded as among the first-fruits of the promise found in Psalm 68:31 (Acts 8). The third example of an individual coming under the influence of the Messiah (chapter 10) appears to be an adumbration of the final episode of Acts which is located in Rome. The centre-piece within the triad indicates Luke's main interest in the former Semitic zealot who became the chief agent in carrying the evangel beyond the borders of Palestine into the very centre of the evil Empire. Saul of Tarsus, then, becomes for Luke the best example of a person who has fully committed herself or himself to the redemptive and imposing Messianic Presence whose power is mediated through the Pentecostal Spirit. This fact can be easily borne out by the amount of space (an estimated two-thirds of Luke's material) dedicated to the apostle. From chapter 13 to the end, then, Paul has been Luke's hero.

[172]Chapt. 9 records the conversion of an Asian, the apostle to Gentiles and Jews. For the significance of the Eunuch's salvation for Luke's purpose, see Beverley Roberts Gaventa, "Whatever Happened to Those Prophesying Daughters?" in *A Feminist Companion to the Acts of the Apostles*, ed. Amy-Jill Levine, with Marriane Blickenstaff (Cleveland, Ohio: Pilgrim Press, 2004), 57; and especially Mickeal Parson, *Body and Character in Luke and Acts: The Subversion of Physiognomy in Early Christianity* (Grand Rapids: Baker Academic, 2006), 123-142).

CHAPTER 8

[173] Rouven Genz, Jesaja 53 als theologische Mitte der Apostelgeschichte: Studien zu ihrer Christologie und Ekklesiologie im Anschluss an Apg 8,26-40 Tübingen: Mohr Siebeck, 2015. [Original title]

[174] This review was published by RBL ã2018 by the Society of Biblical Literature. For more information on obtaining a subscription to RBL, please visit http://www.bookreviews.org/subscribe.asp.

[175] Another statement of the ubiquitous NT 'I' is located in this chapter. At the start of the chapter, we are informed of the burial of Stephen, and the persecution that ensued against the Jerusalem church. We are also told of how they who were scattered became bold in spreading the good news. Luke particularly singled out one of Stephen's companions who went to Samaria to carry out his work of evangelism. While there he received further marching orders to go South. There he encountered an Ethiopian on his way home from Jerusalem, reading from an Isaiah scroll. Philip, the evangelist, inquired of him if he understood the chapter from which he was, apparently, reading aloud. Philip's question elicited another from the African (Πῶς γὰρ ἂν δυναίμην ἐὰν μή τις ὁδηγήσει με; How can I except someone should guide me?). Luke then 'interrupts' or slows down the narrative by citing some 'verses 'from the LXX: 32 ἡ δὲ περιοχὴ τῆς γραφῆς ἣν ἀνεγίνωσκεν ἦν αὕτη· Ὡς πρόβατον ἐπὶ σφαγὴν ἤχθη, καὶ ὡς ἀμνὸς ἐναντίον τοῦ κείραντος αὐτὸν ἄφωνος, οὕτως οὐκ ἀνοίγει τὸ στόμα αὐτοῦ. 33 ἐν τῇ ταπεινώσει ἡ κρίσις αὐτοῦ ἤρθη· τὴν γενεὰν αὐτοῦ τίς διηγήσεται; ὅτι αἴρεται ἀπὸ τῆς γῆς ἡ ζωὴ αὐτοῦ. At this point, Luke records a third question (34 ἀποκριθεὶς δὲ ὁ εὐνοῦχος τῷ Φιλίππῳ εἶπεν· Δέομαί σου, περὶ τίνος ὁ προφήτης λέγει τοῦτο; περὶ ἑαυτοῦ ἢ περὶ ἑτέρου τινός;). Both questions on the part of the African have I-statements (δυναίμην; Δέομαί).[175] They both help to highlight the questioner's innocence and humility, and they both stand in contrast to another in the chapter whose character is revealed in part by an I-locution (v. 19; ἐπιθῶ).

CHAPTER 9

The Austere Asian

1-22 IF THE AFRICAN IN THE previous chapter was a Jewish 'proselyte,' the European of the next chapter a God fearer, the man in this chapter is undoubtedly a zealot of no mean order. He was there in chapter 6 witnessing the murder of Stephen. He is now on his way to Syria to arrest adherents (both sisters and brothers!) of the *Way* (cf. John 14:16) to make them pay. He is in for a rude awakening (1-3)! "Having fallen to the ground, he heard a voice saying, 'Saul, Saul why are you persecuting *me'?*"[176] "Who are you Lord?" is the somewhat confused response of Saul. Then comes the revelation! "I am Jesus whom you persecute; v. 5b).[177] Barrett sums up the significance of verse 5 in this way:

The question corresponds to the ["I am," ἐγώ εἰμι/*egō eimi*] that follows. Saul is aware that he is confronted by a superhuman being; . . . The question leads to identification: the superhuman stranger is Jesus . . . The discovery that the crucified Jesus was in fact alive agrees with Paul's own account of the origin of his Christian life (Gal. 1:15, 16; Cor 9:1; 15: 8; CF. Phil. 3:7-11), and was the root of the new understanding of the OT and the reinterpretation of Judaism that were the foundation of his theology.[178]

For the first time Saul of Taurus is now receiving orders from the very Master he was in the habit of persecuting ignorantly (6). If he became a child of God on this very day, we should notice that the call of salvation and the call to serve are virtually one and the same for him.

The men travelling with Saul heard a voice but did not see anyone; if Saul glimpsed the Lord of glory, he was soon blinded by the light of glory that surrounded Jesus (7-8).[179] After that he was without sight and without food for three days. But Saul had from that day onwards the Light of the world and the Bread of life forever; for the rest of his days, he would share the Light, mostly among gentiles (v 9).

But before all of that the former persecutor, prosecutor, and police of the church needs help to prepare him for the arduous task ahead; so the Lord calls upon a Syrian servant to begin, or better, continue (for Saul was already praying), the process of spiritual rehabilitation (10-11). Ananias' response, though somewhat laughable,[180] is understandable (12-14[181]).

CHAPTER 9

In verses 15-16 the Lord does not engage Ananias in any long conversation about his genuine concerns; Jesus simply re-issues his command,[182] with added details. Ananias complies. Like the three thousand one hundred and twenty in chapter 2, the church in chapter 4, and the deacons in chapter 6, Saul is now ready to serve the Lord under the full sway and strength of the Holy Spirit.

Interestingly, Saul apparently became a child of God in verse 5, was blessed for the first time by the Spirit's control in verse 17,[183] and was immersed in the following verse! Not even the fullness of the Spirit is any substitute for food and fellowship; but without it both fellowship and food lose their significance (19). It is evidently the Spirit's power that enabled Saul to proclaim Jesus as the Son of God and Messiah, to the amazement of the Syrian audience (20-22).

23-31 But the success of these early days as an evangelist did not last too long (23-24). If some of Moses' early days were spent in an African basket, another prophetic successor will do the same in Asia over a thousand years after (25). After the basket experience, Saul headed south to attend church, but the disciples of Christ were petrified at his presence. Seven or so days ago Ananias felt the same way. It took divine revelation to change his mind—and emotion. There is no such revelation in Jerusalem. This time God simply moved Joseph the son of consolation to save the day.

It was only in this way that Saul was able to resume his ministry started in Damascus. If his efforts in the Syrian city were risky, Jerusalem will fare no better. As a result of all of this Saul was enabled to visit his 'Turkish' home town once again (26-30). In his absence, the people of God had rest from the man who made them restless (31: "Then the church throughout Judea, Galilee[184] and Samaria enjoyed a time of peace and was strengthened. Living in the fear of the Lord and encouraged by the Holy Spirit, it increased in numbers"—The Message); yet Saul himself got very little rest for the rest of his life.

32-43 A broad biographical outline of the book of Acts foregrounds both Peter (1-11) and Paul (12-28). But of course, chapter 9 provides us with a beautiful overlap of the ministries of the two outstanding apostles in Luke's second volume.

So while Saul withdraws from the scene for the time being, Peter takes centre stage once again. At Pentecost he was used by God to permanently heal about three thousand souls; in chapters 3-5, he was engaged in other healing encounters. Here in verses 32-43, he continues in the therapeutic steps of the Master, including the raising of the dead.

---

[176] *"Saal, Saal, wai yu mek mi sofa?"* (v.4). Saul immediately responded: *"Uu yu, Laad?"* (v. 5a) Then came the surprising rejoinder: *"Mi a Jiizas, di wan we yu a mek sofa"* (v. 5b; **JNT**).

[177] Like in chapter 7:7 and 32, this saying (Ἐγώ εἰμι Ἰησοῦς ὃν σὺ διώκεις) is buttressed by the independent first person pronoun. The event is so significant for Luke's narrative that it is repeated twice, each in its own peculiar context (chapters 22 and 26).

[178] Barrett, *Acts*, 450; cf. Bock, *Acts*, 349, 354-362.

[179] Is the opening of the eyes (v 8) a *double entendre* (i.e., both spiritually and physically)? D B Martin (*Biblical Truths* [New Haven

and London: Yale, 2017], 15) feels that Saul was not converted, in the sense of giving up Judaism for Christianity; but see Gal 1, Phil 3, and 1 Cor 9:19-21.

[180] As if the Lord does not watch the latest news or check FB regularly!

[181] Here (14) the new people of God are called those who invoke the name of the glorified Messiah and saints in v. 13; in v.10 one of them is simply a disciple.

[182] ἐγὼ γὰρ ὑποδείξω αὐτῷ (*for I-n-I shall show him*) is emphatic.

[183] This verse is touching ("brother Saul") and arresting; Saul is in Damascus to lay hands on the disciples. Instead, a disciple lay hands on him to advance a different cause.

[184] On this, consult the relevant article in *ABD*.

CHAPTER 10

The Exemplary European

1-33 THERE IS A SPIRITUAL PRINCIPLE that goes like this: light received brings more light. Light rejected brings only night. The negative side of this equation is richly illustrated in Romans 1-3, where the *Heathen, Hypocrite, Hebrew* and, in a word, all humanity are castigated for ignoring the lit-candle (*general revelation*), the bulb (*special revelation*), and the Son-light (*quintessential revelation*).

The Cornelius narrative illustrates what happens when someone—anyone!—accepts the light graciously given from above. In Cornelius's case, two messengers were sent to him: one from heaven and one from below (1-8). For him, more light is on its way.[185]

So, about noon on the following day, while Cornelius's men were on their way to the city, Peter made his way to the roof in order to pray. Feeling hungry just at the time when a meal was being prepared downstairs, he fell into a trance and saw a large sheet being lowered from heaven with all types of quadruped, crawling animals and birds. After this a voice said: "Peter, get up, kill and eat!" "No way, Lord," Peter responded, "I have never eaten non-kosher food." (9-14).

Preachers like to remind us: "If you say 'Lord' you can't say in the same breath, 'not so!'" But the voice from above is patient, kind, and longsuffering. So the One from above speaks a second time (15), and the audio-visual lesson continues (16).

In the Gospels, particularly the Gospel of Mark, we see that even with the best teacher, students do not get it. Verses 17-18 demonstrate that even with the best multi-media presentation—and the indwelling Spirit—we still sometimes don't get it. So the Spirit seeks to clarify matters and further directs (19). But the Spirit's speaking and clarification is not always incompatible with human intervention (20-23).

All this led to a meeting with Cornelius the exemplary Roman, Peter the Pentecostal preacher, and a much smaller audience than the one we encounter in chapter three (24-27). After the exchange of how they were providentially brought together, Peter finally got it (well not quite!).[186] And then he begins the proclamation of his gospel conviction (28-43).

> And he said to them, *Ye* know how it is unlawful for a Jew to be joined or come to one of a strange race, and to *me* God has shewn to call no man common or unclean.

CHAPTER 10

²⁹ Wherefore also, having been sent for, I came without saying anything against it. I inquire therefore for what reason ye have sent for me.³⁰ And Cornelius said, Four days ago I had been [fasting] unto this hour, and the ninth [I was] praying in my house, and lo, a man stood before me in bright clothing, ³¹ and said, Cornelius, thy prayer has been heard, and thy alms have come in remembrance before God.

³² Send therefore to Joppa and fetch Simon, who is surnamed Peter; he lodges in the house of Simon, a tanner, by the sea [who when he is come will speak to thee]. ³³ Immediately therefore I sent to thee, and *thou* hast well done in coming. Now therefore *we* are all present before God to hear all things that are commanded thee of God. ³⁴ And Peter opening his mouth said, "Of a truth I perceive that God is no respecter of persons, ³⁵ but in every nation he that fears him and works righteousness is acceptable to him." ³⁶ The word which he sent to the sons of Israel, preaching peace by Jesus Christ, (*he* is Lord of all things,)

³⁷ *Ye* know; the testimony which has spread through the whole of Judaea, beginning from Galilee after the baptism which John preached—³⁸ Jesus who [was] of Nazareth: how God anointed him with [the] Holy Spirit and with power; who went through [all quarters] doing good, and healing all that were under the power of the devil, because God was with him. ³⁹ *We* also [are] witnesses of all things which he did both in the country of the Jews and in Jerusalem; whom they also slew, having hanged him on a cross.⁴⁰ This [man] God raised up the third day and gave him to be openly seen, ⁴¹ not of all the people, but of witnesses who were chosen before of God, *us* who have eaten and drunk with him after he arose from among [the] dead.

⁴² And he commanded us to preach to the people, and to testify that *he* it is who was determinately appointed of God [to be] judge of living and dead. ⁴³ To him all the prophets bear witness that every one that believes on him will receive through his name remission of sins (DV).

Before Peter was through with his message, a mini-Pentecost was in the making. Peter and his entourage witnessed for themselves Gentiles receiving the Spirit, speaking in tongues, and their being immersed in the name of Christ Jesus (44-48). So far in the book of Acts we have seen people tarrying for the Spirit (1:5), identifying themselves with the name of Jesus to receive the Spirit (2:38), having hands laid on them for the Spirit's anointing (chapters 8 and 9), and now in this chapter people are baptized[187] by the Spirit before the conclusion of the sermon!

All this begs the question: Which of these experiences is normative today? There is no definitive answer from Dr Luke. Another question begs itself: What is the normative (if any) accompanying sign of the Spirit's initial presence in the believer's life—speaking in tongues, prophesying, sound of a hurricane, laying on of hands, prayer, cloven tongues of fire?

Only one thing seems certain (according to Luke's travelling companion); without the indwelling Spirit in my life I don't belong to Christ (Rom 5:5; 8:9). Another thing is certain: Peter was asked to tarry in the final verse of this chapter! To summarize, in the three crucial chapters ending with this one:

CHAPTER 10

We see the divine initiative to salvage and purify the three streams of humanity through the Gospel: a representative Hamite in chapter 8, a Semite in chapter 9, and a Japhethite in chapter 10.[188] What this suggests to us is that cultural revitalisation is best preceded by new theological thinking, which in turn is totally dependent on special revelation/or intervention. Rightly it is said that we were made by God, and therefore all our problems are theological. Henceforth, all lasting solutions have theological roots as well.[189]

---

[185] V. 4 seems to support the idea that God definitely answers the prayers of sincere unbelievers as part of his goodness that leads to repentance (Rom 2) "Your prayers," replied the angel, ". . . have gone up into God's presence, so that he has you on his mind" (Complete Jewish Bible).

[186] See Galatians 2.

[187] Can you imagine! In "January 5, 1527: Swiss Anabaptist reformer Felix Manz is drowned in punishment for preaching adult baptism, becoming the first Protestant martyred by other Protestants." https://www.christianitytoday.com/history/today/january-5.html.

[188] Schnabel (*Early Christian Mission*, vol. 2, [Deerfield, ILL: IVP, 2004], 297-299) argues that Paul's mission was primarily to the Japhetites; in his commentary on Acts (423, n.5), he cites the outline of another scholar: "[T]he mission to Shem is described in Acts 2:1-8:25 . . . Ham 8:26-40 . . . Japheth 9:1-28:31."

[189] https://biblicalstudies.org.uk/pdf/cjet/07_078.pdf p. 89.

CHAPTER 11

VERSES 1-18 CONSTITUTE A virtual repetition of the previous chapter; essentially it is Peter testimony.[190]

19-21 It seems as if the writer goes out of his way to present the church of Antioch as the new model church (cf. 2:42ff). But before he does so, he informs of the circumstances surrounding the planting of this assembly—the first outside the so-called Holy Land.

Sent Disciples (19-21)

Now those who had been scattered by the persecution that broke out when Stephen was killed travelled as far as Phoenicia, Cyprus and Antioch, spreading the word only among Jews. [20] Some of them, however, men from Cyprus and Cyrene, went to Antioch and began to speak to Greeks also, telling them the good news about the Lord Jesus. [21] The Lord's hand was with them, and a great number of people believed and turned to the Lord.

The martyrdom of Stephen and the ensuing persecution had far-reaching effects: 1) ordinary believers are engaged in the process of evangelisation (cf. 1:8; 8:1-4); 2) the gospel reaches the Samaritans (8:5ff); and 3) now the ancestors of Lebanon (*Phoenicia*), the Isle of Cyprus, as well as Syrians (from the city of *Antioch*) have the wonderful opportunity to be saved (21).

Spirit-Filled Disciples (22-24)

²² News of this reached the church in Jerusalem, and they sent Barnabas to Antioch. ²³ When he arrived and saw what the grace of God had done, he was glad and encouraged them all to remain true to the Lord*¹⁹¹* with all their hearts. ²⁴ He was a good man, full of the Holy Spirit and faith, and a great number of people were brought to the Lord.

In these verses only Barnabas is said to be controlled by Spirit. However, the response of the mother church in sending one of their best is nothing short of that divine experience (22), and Barnabas, the generous and faithful man of God, did not disappoint (23-24).¹⁹²

Sturdy Disciples (25-26)

²⁵ Then Barnabas went to Tarsus to look for Saul, ²⁶ and when he found him, he brought him to Antioch. So, for a whole year Barnabas and Saul met with the church and taught great numbers of people. The disciples were called Christians first at Antioch.

Barnabas' total dependence on the Spirit at this point is also made manifest by his genuine humility (put another way, lack of insecurity) in seeking help; his strength apparently is counselling and evangelism (vv 24-24). He could teach as well. But he knew someone who could probably do it better. May be the task was too much for one man to bear. So he sought help (25).

As a result of the concerted effort of solid Bible teaching by Barnabas and company (and the obedience of the people! Cf. Matt 28:19-20), there was evident behavioural modification, and a new name for the people of the Way (26). Even the great apostle Peter (*Primus inter partes*) [193] approved of it!

Sacrificial Disciples (27-30)

²⁷ During this time some prophets came down from Jerusalem to Antioch. ²⁸ One of them, named Agabus, stood up and through the Spirit predicted that a severe famine would spread over the entire Roman world. (This happened during the reign of Claudius.) ²⁹ The disciples, as each one was able, decided to provide help for the brothers and sisters living in Judea. ³⁰ This they did, sending their gift to the elders by Barnabas and Saul.

Sometime after Barnabas was again sent north to Syria, while other members of the Jerusalem congregation made their way to the same church to warn the believers of a serious season of testing that was to come upon the Empire (27-28).

The response of the Antiochan Christians was nothing short of stunning; it's like all the members of the Anglophone Caribbean deciding to help the UK in their approaching famine of God's word (resulting from a postmodern stance against the gospel of Christ?) or to a lesser extent, another dire situation that would necessitate another 'Windrush' to rebuild the country (29-30).

---

[190] The testimony begins with an independent first person pronoun and ends with another; they both add rhetorical flourish and conviction to the testimony: Ἐγὼ ἤμην ἐν πόλει Ἰόππῃ προσευχόμενος καὶ εἶδον ἐν ἐκστάσει ὅραμα (5; see also vv 6, 7, 8, 16, 17).

[191] The joy of this counselor par excellence, as well as his wisdom of instruction is exemplary.

[192] Verse 21 (The Lord's hand was with them, and a great number of people believed and turned to the Lord) and v. 24b (and a great number of people were brought to the Lord) seem to form an inclusio. There's also a ring composition somewhere: **A**-The Lord; **B**-great number; **B¹**-great number; **A¹**-The Lord.

[193] First among equals.

CHAPTER 12

1-5 VERSES 1-2 INTRODUCE a particularly trying season for the church. One of the first century I-Three (Peter, James, and John) is murdered by an arrogant politician. How could God allow something like this to happen? Luke provides us with no answer to this question (but cf. 2:23!). However, in the Third Gospel he catalogues the worst case of injustice and murder known to man (that of his Lord and Saviour) and champions the cause that this event is the key to optimum human flourishing in this life and the next (Luke 19:10; 23:34, 39-43).

It would appear that very few politicians have the will power to resist the urge to merely please the people instead of standing up for what is right and just. Herod was one such. So, Peter is arrested also.[194] Years earlier the resurrected Lord predicted the last days of Peter and, to a lesser extent, John (John 21). On that occasion nothing was said about James. Here in this chapter, we see what Jesus could have said about the dearly departed. Will Peter meet the same fate?[195] Yes, but not in Palestine; and not in the prime of his life. Not when the people of God are praying (3-5). He will experience old age.

6-19 The answer to their prayer was fast asleep like Jonah (Jonah 1). I still wonder how Peter managed to close his eyes in that environment; the sleep was so sweet that he hardly realized that what was happening was real. But finally he came to his senses (6-11). By this time the heavenly messenger leaves the 'inmate', and he heads for the gathering of prayer warriors. But how much faith is behind the worthwhile exercise? On account of unbelief the answer to their prayer is left standing at the entrance (12-14).

Verse 15 seems tragic and comical at the same time. The 'angel' Rhoda announced that God had granted a positive response to their intercession and supplication. They now conclude that she is out of her mind! But in fairness to them, sometimes the answers to our prayers appear too good to be true.

The earthly angel insists she is in her right mind. They have another tentative conclusion (16-17). The angel (Rhoda) must have seen Peter's angel. Alas, they finally dismissed their hypotheses (the first psychological and the second theological) and embraced the solid rock of truth nicknamed Peter (16). One wonders how many of us believers twenty centuries removed from Peter's drama are able to recognize the answers to our own petitions.

But back to the first century: Peter recounts how he was miraculously rescued from certain death. This, no doubt, was cause for much rejoicing (17). Meanwhile instead of celebration, the following couple of verses speak of consternation and condemnation leading to death (18-19). So

CHAPTER 12

the one responsible for the deaths of James—the first to go to heaven from the original apostolic band—and some of his own, will die an ugly death, not a judicial action from Peter's 'angel', but from one mightier than he (20-23).

Neither the death of Herod nor the 'sleep' of James adversely affected the spread of the word. In fact, the passing of the latter may have very well aided and abetted that spread, since the blood of the martyrs is the seed of the church.[196] One more thing: whereas wealthy king Herod joined the rich man, penniless James had to make common cause with poor Lazarus (Luke 16).[197]

---

[194] The Jews were pleased with the death of James. The political murderer was more than pleased with his work and hastened to kill Peter. But God had other plans; he stirred his people to pray (v 5). The first answer to prayer was sleep after the order of Adam (Gen 2; Psa 127).

[195] According to reliable tradition, he was executed in Rome by Nero.

[196] http://www.earlychurchtexts.com/public/tertullian_blood_christians_seed.htm.

[197] Reminiscent of a statement attributed to Bishop Desmond Tutu: "When the white man came to Africa they taught us to sing, 'Take the whole world but give me Jesus'. Now they have taken the whole world and left us with Jesus. Now we will see who have the better deal."

CHAPTER 13

1-15 BOTH MEN WERE ALREADY missionaries, and both were given new assignments through the agency of the Spirit and the blessing of their assembly. So, Barnabas and Saul:

> sent on their way by the Holy Spirit, went down to Seleucia and sailed from there to Cyprus. ⁵ When they arrived at Salamis,[198] they proclaimed the word of God in the Jewish synagogues. John was with them as their helper. ⁶ They travelled through the whole island until they came to Paphos. . .¹³ From Paphos, Paul and his companions sailed to Perga in Pamphylia, where John left them to return to Jerusalem. ¹⁴ From Perga they went on to Pisidian Antioch.[199] On the Sabbath they entered the synagogue and sat down. ¹⁵ After the reading from the Law and the Prophets, the leaders of the synagogue sent word to them, saying, "Brothers, if you have a word of exhortation for the people, please speak." (13:4-15).[200]

ACTS

Above, Luke introduced his first transcript[201] of Paul's gospel proclamation to a group. Ten more are to follow; they are as follows: to Gentiles (14:15-18; 17:22-31), Christians (20:17-38), Jews (22:1-21; 23:1-6), Gentiles (24:10-21; 25:8-11; 26:1-23), Jews (28:17-20; 25-28).[202] But before we look at the one below, a survey of the chapter is in order.

We understand from the opening verses that the church of Antioch was apparently like the one in Achaia in the sense that "they came behind in no gifts" (1 Cor 1:7). Only teachers and prophets are mentioned in verse 1 but we can be certain that they were other gifted people in Antioch as well. The leadership, at least, was quite diverse; it has representatives hailing from the island of Cyrus (Barnabas), and parts of Africa (Simeon and Lucius).

But the most important thing about these leaders is their piety. Their pious posture before God enabled them to hear from God and be willing to release two of their choicest servants:

> [2] While they were worshiping the Lord and fasting, the Holy Spirit[203] said, "Set apart for me Barnabas and Saul for the work to which I have called them." [3] So after they had fasted and prayed, they placed their hands on them and sent them off (NIV).

So off they went to the home town of Barnabas, Cyprus. Almost immediately they began proclaiming the word at Salamis. Fully conversant with the law of fishing, they began their ministry where there are gatherings of

CHAPTER 13

Jews. It is said that if you are witnessing to Gentile Americans, you go from house to house; to American Jews? You go from store to store. In the Caribbean it is probably best done after a football match.[204]

John Mark was also a part of the touring delegation. But was he called? Yes, but not in the manner of his senior partners Barnabas and Saul. Not all calls are dramatic; but the call of John is no less a defining moment in his life (4-5).

The team will then traverse the entire island of Cyprus, encountering opposition and a setback along the way (6-13), but also making the best of their opportunities (14-48[205]). So

> The word of the Lord spread through the whole region. [50] But the Jewish leaders incited the God-fearing women of high standing and the leading men of the city. They stirred up persecution against Paul and Barnabas, and expelled them from their region. [51] So they shook the dust off their feet as a warning to them and went to Iconium. [52] And the disciples were filled with joy and with the Holy Spirit (NIV).

---

[198] A note of further interest is that both visited their respective home town early in their missionary career, Saul to Tarsus and Barnabas to Cyprus.

[199] "In the heart of present-day Turkey, according to Paul Ellington, "Acts 13.38," *The Bible Translator* 45 (April 1994): 242.

[200] Were they familiar with the Jesus tradition which likens evangelism to the catching of fish? Implied in the metaphor is the thought that the best way to catch fish is to go to their natural habitat. The syn-

agogue in those days was the best place to reach Jews, proselytes and God-fearing Gentiles.

[201] The transcript contains seven I-statements. The first is in verse 22. Like Peter's sermon in chapter 2, Paul quotes Scripture to bolster his argument, and like Stephen's speech he recites Jewish history. The quotation is from 1 Sam 13:14.

[202] Adapted from Eckhard J. Schnabel, *Acts: Exegetical Commentary on the New Testament* (Grand Rapids: Zondervan, 2012), 552. For assessments of the discourses in general and one in Southern Galatia in particular, see respectively, W. Gasque, "The Speeches in Acts," in R.N. Longenecker and M. Tenney, eds., *New Dimensions in NT Study* (Grand Rapids: Zondervan, 1974), 232-250; and "Mission and Misunderstanding: Paul and Barnabas in Lystra" (Acts 14: 18-20) in Anthony Billington et al., eds., *Mission and Meaning: Essays Presented to Peter Cotterell* (Carlisle, UK: Paternoster, 1995), 56-69.

[203] See W C van Unnick, *Sparsa Collecta*, pt.2 (Leiden: Brill, 1980), 323-332.

[204] See Appendix 2.

[205] "The present verse is as unqualified a statement of absolute predestination —'the eternal purpose of God' (Calvin 393) —as is found anywhere in the NT. Those believed who were appointed (the passive implies, by God) to do so. The rest, one infers, did not believe, did not receive eternal life, and were thus appointed to death. The positive statement implies the negative. This can hardly be avoided by saying, with Schmithals (127) that what we have here is not Prädestinationslehre [a doctrine of predestination] but Ebrauungssprache [edification talk]." (C.K. Barrett, *Acts vol.1*[London: T &T Clark, 1994], 658).

CHAPTER 14

1-10 THERE IS FURTHER SUCCESS at Iconium, as well as further setback (1-2). The missioners, however, did not allow the latter to dampen their spirit (3). Their resolve divided the masses, causing more problems for them. At this point they must have recalled an important oral tradition recorded in the first Synoptic volume (Matt 10:19-20; cf. Luke 12:11-12); their obedience turned out to be a blessing for the people of Lystra and Derbe (4-10).

The blessing bestowed deserves more than a thank you note, but in a context of gross idolatry and superstition the humble missionaries got more than they bargained for! What do servants of the living and true God do in such a situation? The truth is their only defence (11-18):

> In past generations He allowed all the nations to go their own way, [17] although He did not leave Himself without a witness, since He did what is good by giving you rain from heaven and fruitful seasons and satisfying your hearts with food and happiness." [18] Even though they said these things, they barely stopped the crowds from sacrificing to them (HCSB).

CHAPTER 14

19-28 Remember the saying, "Life is hard and then you die"? I doubt that these missionaries knew it; certainly, they were familiar with the philosophy behind it—and we are glad they did not buy into it. As another saying goes, "You just can't keep a good man down," whether for three minutes, three hours or, like Someone Paul knows quite well, three days (19-20).

Despite the hic-cups, the missionary duo continues to engage in the good works their Master had ordained for them (cf. Eph. 2:10)—particularly evangelisation and edification (21-22). If the ultimate goal of their mission is to plant churches that are self-supporting (like Antioch), self-propagating (like Jerusalem), then local leaders must be identified and appointed for the fledgling assembly to become self-governing (23). Having done that, Barnabas and his worthy companion embarked upon a rigorous return trip, passing through "Pisidia[206] and . . . Pamphylia" (24).

> [25] After they spoke the message in Perga,[207] they went down to Attalia. [26] From there they sailed back to Antioch where they had been entrusted to the grace of God for the work they had now completed. [27] After they arrived and gathered the church together, they reported everything God had done with them and that He had opened the door of faith to the Gentiles. [28] And they spent a considerable time with the disciples.

So all's well that ends well—for the time being (25-28).

207, P. Stuhlmacher, *Biblical Theology of the NT* (Grand Rapids: Eerdmans, 2018), 256.

CHAPTER 15

VERSE 1 SETS THE AGENDA for this crucial passage. Put another way: By what ethical code will the new people of God be guided; and on what is their salvation grounded? The Pharisaic faction in the church stoutly maintained the viability of the Mosaic code of ethics as well as its salvific relevance, while Barnabas, Paul, Peter, and James oppose it.

The passage[208] on a whole:

> Relates... how the early church reached a consensus decision regarding the disputed question of whether Gentile Christians should submit to circumcision and to the wholesale obedience to the Mosaic law. The passage states (with Peter) that faith in Jesus and the grace of the Lord are the basis for salvation.

It states (Paul and Barnabas) that God has authenticated the Gentile mission in which Gentiles are not told to become Jewish proselytes. And it states (James) that Gentile Christians are members of God's people *as Gentiles* [italics Schnabel's], worshipping God in the temple . . ., which is the messianic community of the last days, and that Gentile Christians need to comply only with some fundamental regulations that the law stipulated for Gentiles living among Jews.[209]

Schnabel continues:

> The episode . . . is made up of eight incidents. Luke relates the prehistory of the meeting in Jerusalem . . . (vv. 1-3). The Antioch delegation arrives, with a report of Paul and Barnabas (vv. 4-5). The apostles and elders convene a council meeting . . . (vv. 6-7a). Peter gives a speech . . . (vv. 7b-11). . . Paul and Barnabas report about their missionary work . . . (v.12). James gives a speech (vv. 13-21) that confirms the theological consensus . . . The decision of the assembly ("the apostolic decree") is recorded in a letter (vv. 22-29). Luke ends the narrative . . . in Antioch (30-33).

There appears to be another chiastic arrangement within this central C-section (1-33):

A Antioch (v. 1)

B Revelation of the problem by the delegation, apostles and elders (vv2-7a)

   C Peter's speech (7b-11)

D Missionary report featuring the acts of God (v.12)

C´ James' speech (13-21)[210]

B´ Resolution of the problem by the delegation, the apostles and the elders (vv 22-29)

A´ Antioch (30-35)

For Luke, then, even when the missionaries are not carrying out their substantive responsibility, the acts of God in terms of miracles among the Gentiles, take centre-stage. The paradoxical silence of the missionaries for the time being (no evangelisation) brings another kind of silence which seems to echo to echo the solemn affirmation: "Be still and know that I am God."

We now return to the question of the two ethical codes (Mosaic and Messianic) that are at the heart of the discussion at the apostolic council. If this question were not dealt with adequately then there would have been a very different end to the story—not only for Luke's two volumes but also for subsequent ecclesiology and the missiology that drives it. The question is of paramount importance.[211] We continue with a biblical-theological survey of three crucial codes to cement our point.

Right throughout the canon one senses a strong ethical imperative. In both the Old and New Testaments, we see that all of humanity is subject to a ubiquitous ethical imperative, a strong sense of divine ought. Though not explicitly stated, this must have been the basis of the global-flood judgment; the human race at the time was said to be violent and evil.

Ample time was given to them for repentance but there was no behaviour modification. There were murder and bigamy before the flood, and the punishment of these sinful acts assumes an ethical frame of reference that was divinely sanctioned. Sin in every era then is the transgression of an ethical standard. What we are positing here is that this standard is part and parcel of the *imago Dei*.

It is not surprising therefore to find in Genesis an individual called Melchizedek whose commitment to authentic ethical behaviour pattern qualified him, among other things, to function as priest of the Most High God.

It is no surprise either to hear God's word to Isaac that his father "obeyed me and kept my charge, my commandments, my statutes, and my laws" (Genesis 26:5). And given the pre-Israelite background and chronology (twentieth-century BCE) of the protagonist, our understanding of Job 23:12 takes on new significance.

Outside of Scripture, we hear a voice like Epictetus echoing Holy Writ with these wise words: "If a man could only subscribe heart and soul, as he ought, to this doctrine,[212] that we are all primarily begotten of God, and that God is the father of all men . . . I think that he will entertain no ignoble or mean thought about himself."[213] Such laws, we further submit, belong to an ethical system or code that we may call the 'Mesographic Law'.[214]

This Law is given to everyone and is therefore universal in scope (cf. Amos 4:13: "He reveals his will to every person . . ."). Thus an observant atheist can write regarding the Decalogue: "Admonishments of this kind are found in virtually every culture throughout recorded history. . . It is a scientific fact that moral emotions—like a sense of fair play or abhorrence to cruelty—precede any exposure to scripture."[215]

We agree. This innate sense of morality is the basis, for example, of the ethical imperative of thanksgiving[216] which in part provides us with a better understanding of humanity's culpability in Romans 1: 21(they were guilty of ingratitude).²¹⁷

It was this Mesographic revelation that enabled the Greco-Roman philosopher/priest and contemporary of the apostle Paul to have penned the following treatise on deity: "God is unmoved and timeless, in whom there is neither "earlier nor later, no future nor past, no older nor younger; but He, being One . . . has with only one 'Now' completely filled 'Forever.'

Under these conditions, therefore, we ought, as we pay him reverence, to greet him and to address him with these words, 'Thou art'; or even, I vow, as did some of the men of old." ²¹⁸ Similarly, we have the following testimony from Hellenistic Jewry: "[T]hose who dwell on earth shall be tormented, because though they had understanding they committed iniquity, and though they received the commandments they did not keep them, and though they obtained the law they dealt unfaithfully with what they received."²¹⁹

But before the Hellenistic age another Law was given, the famous Mosaic variety. This Law was limited in scope (Psa 147:19-20) but was of much more significance than that which preceded it, since its stipulations (613 of them) set apart all who had a special covenant with Yahweh.

So how does this Mosaic variety relate to its Mesographic counterpart? "The moral law in its written [Mosaic/Messianic?] form does not contradict or change the will of God. Rather, it makes it explicit and amplifies that will as originally expressed in natural law [Mesographic]. Since the will of God does not change, the law remains virtually the same throughout redemptive history."[220]

The Old Testament which implicitly and explicitly informs us about the Mesographic and Mosaic codes of ethics also points to another system in Jeremiah 31: 31-37. Like its predecessor, this new system, far superior to the others, is also tied to a covenant (Matt 26: 26-29). Based on Galatians 6:2 (cf. "rule" v. 16 of the same chapter) and 1 Corinthians 9:19-21 we are justified in classifying this variety the Messianic Law (MeL).

MeL is promulgated, circulated, and has come to be understood as "my commands" (John 14:15), "the perfect law of liberty" (James 1: 25),[221] "that pattern of teaching to [which] you were entrusted" (Rom 6:17 NET), "dominical directive" (1 Cor 14: 37, our translation), "the commands of God" (Rev 14:12),[222] as well as the "but I [*egō*] say on to you" refinements of the Sermon on the Mount.

In all of these NT genres the ethical imperative is evident. MeL was first announced by Jeremiah 31:31-37 (cf. Isa 55:3; Eze 16:60), and even a fragment from the Qumran community (4Q521) appears to anticipate it, ". . . [the hea]vens and the earth will listen to His Messiah, and none therein will stray from *the commandments* of the holy ones[*qᵉdôsîm*]."[223]

So where in the book of Acts do we find evidence of such a code of ethics? Chapter 1 with its dominical directives to wait (in prayer?) in Jerusalem for the coming of the Spirit, and to witness to the world, along with the devotedness of the three-thousand strong to the apostolic *didache* (chapt 2:42) all point in that direction.

The resolve of the apostles to give themselves to prayer and proclamation in chapter 6 seems to be another example. The Jerusalem Council (JC), with its strategic placement in the narrative, should not be overlooked in this regard. The rhetoric of 15:11 is a timely reminder that there is a new Lord who is "large and in charge."

If the early disciples are devoted to the apostle's teaching (chapter 2:42a), as we have seen above, the missionaries (to Antioch in chapter 11; from Antioch in chapter 13) were no less committed to the "name of our Lord Jesus Christ" (15:26b).

Who can doubt that the mention of Barnabas and Paul in such a manner is paradigmatic? One wonders as well if the statements concerning the salvific grace of the lord in verse 15:11, supernatural acts of God in verse 15:12, and the shared goodness of the Spirit in verse 15:28 are not theologically pregnant.

Almost any reading of capter15, then, leaves the impression that the Messianic lordship and law (seen as a unit) is prominent and pre-eminent, and the Mosaic law which bears witness to it is to be seen as a backdrop—an important backdrop to the drama of redemption mind you—but should never be foregrounded in any shape or form.[224] Both the mountain setting (reminiscent of Sinai?) and the magisterial statement of Luke 9:28-36 point in the same direction: the Messianic law replaces the mosaic.

In this way the book of Acts (and the mission it promotes) is in sync with the other documents that make up the literature of the new covenant. In sum, the three codes of ethics that govern the world look like this:

| Mesographic Code | Mosaic Code |
| Romans 2:12-15 | Psalm 147:19-20 |

Primarily for every Gentile[225]   Primarily for every Jew

| Messianic Code |
| 1 Corinthians 9:19-23 |

Primarily for every Christian[226]

Interestingly, from a historical perspective the first (mesographic) code is tied to creation as a necessary component of the image of God; the last (Messianic) is intimately connected to the new creation (cf. 2 Cor 5:17). Both the first and the last are written within (Rom 2:14-15; Jer 31: 31-33, respectively). It is the second that is written on stone, possibly suggesting its interim character.

All three codes, it is to be noted, have the same Parent and constitute a graphic triplet. This accounts for their strong resemblance. That there are differences among the three 'sisters' no one denies. The difficulty is to work out how much continuity or discontinuity there is between the Mosaic that gladly plays the role of a John the Baptist in pointing to the Messiah (cf. Luke 24:13-49) and the Messianic which underscores the importance of the former (Matt 5:17-21).

The way Luke's companion handles matters of a sacred day[227] and strict diet in Romans 14 is quite instructive in this regard. Nothing is wrong to observe the Sabbath[228] or to pay close attention to one's diet as it is informed by the relevant principles of the Old Covenant documents. Once the council members were able to have a consensus on the centrality and cruciality of the Messianic categorical, they had no qualms in expressing the sentiments of 15: 28-29.

With this the mission delineated in 1:8 can resume with clearer lines of integrity and conviction, for the Messianic code (unlike its typological predecessors) not only sends (evangelisation); it is also the main basis of the process of strengthening believers new and old (edification).

36-40 So the dynamic duo decides to carry on their ministry along the sure lines of Messianic contours (36). But there's a hurdle of inter-personal challenge to get across; Barnabas, the man who brought Saul into mainstream Christianity at the time, again displays his magnanimous spirit by suggesting that his cousin John Mark be given a second chance.

Paul, the initiator of this second missionary journey, must have uttered something like, "Not over my dead body!" (37-38). "They had a sharp disagreement,[229] so that they parted company. Barnabas took along Mark and sailed away to Cyprus, but Paul chose Silas and set out, commended to the grace of the Lord by the brothers and sisters. He passed through Syria and Cilicia, strengthening the churches (39-41, NET).

Was it nepotism on the part of Barnabas to have elected John? Was Paul too harsh on that occasion, not to have seriously considered the suggestion? All we know at this point is that divine providence[230] (not serendipity!) won the day in the sense that, whereas we had one missionary team, we now have two.

It's a pity though that the career of Barnabas is not followed through; which raises another question: Is Luke so biased to sacrifice the historical memory of Joseph the counsellor par excellence for that of his friend Paul? The latter, in his maturing years, did eventually commend Mark (2 Tim 4:11).

---

[208]"It is not by chance that the Apostolic Council occupies the middle of the book"; Hans Conzelmann, *Acts of the Apostles* (Philadelphia: Fortress, 1987), 115. We concur. Fitzmyer (*The Acts of the Apostles* [New York: Doubleday, 1998], 538) supports the centrality of the pericope by pointing out that both the sections that precede and succeed chapter 15 have approximately 1,200 words. Ibid. On this section (encompassing chapters 13 and 17) and its fruitfulness, see N T Wright, *The Resurrection of the Son of God* (Minneapolis: Fortress, 2003), 450-457.

[209]Eckhard J. Schnabel, *Acts*, 621-622.

[210] "Tannehill [too] notes a neat chiasm in v.16, built around four first-person singular future verbs beginning with the Greek prefix *an-*"; D.G. Peterson, *The Acts of the Apostles*. PNTC (Grand Rapids: Eerdmans, 2009), 431. The construction (with some embellishments) will look something like this:

A   ἀναστρέψω Μετὰ ταῦτα καὶ
    B   ἀνοικοδομήσω τὴν σκηνὴν Δαυὶδ τὴν πεπτωκυῖαν καὶ
    B'   ἀνοικοδομήσω κατεσκαμμένα αὐτῆς καὶ
A'   ἀνορθώσω αὐτήν

[211]M. Dibelius (*The Book of Acts: Form, Style, and Theology* [Minneapolis: Fortress, 2004], 134-139) appears to value the literary

and theological import of the 'Council' but is extremely sceptical of its history.

[212] Gk. *Dogma.*

[213] Epictetus I-II (Cambridge, MA: LCB, 1925), 25. Of course, one has to admit that the echo is faint, since the writer has in mind Zeus and not YHWH. He also writes about what we have called above the mesographic law: "I cannot transgress any of His commands [*entolōn*]. . . . These are the laws [*nomoi*] that have been sent to you from God, these are His ordinances; it is of these you ought to become an interpreter [*exēgētēn*], to these you ought to subject yourself . . ." Idem II: 313.

[214] What Bruce Demarest and Gordon Lewis (Integrative Theology [Grand Rapids: Zondervan, 1996], 1: 95) call 'the implanted law'. Cf. Alan F. Segal ("Paul's Jewish Presuppositions," in *The Cambridge Companion to St Paul* [ed. James Dunn. Cambridge: Cambridge University Press, 2003], 166), who mentions the "seven commandments which the rabbis assumed were given to all humanity before Moses." This universal variety is dubbed 'mesographic', i.e., written inside (cf. Rom. 2:14). We are therefore not surprised at the solemn declaration of Micah 5:15.

[215] Sam Harris, *Letter to a Christian Nation* (NY: Alfred A. Knopf, 2006), 21. See also Simeon McIntosh (*Reading Text & Polity: Hermeneutics and Constitutional Theory* [Kingston: Caribbean Law, 2012], 1): Every "judicial opinion uttered by the judge in the name of the law carries implicitly a claim to moral truth."

[216] Cf. Epictetus, 39, 319: 'From everything that happens in the universe it is easy for a man to find occasion to praise providence, if he has within himself these two qualities: the faculty of taking a comprehensive view of what has happened in each individual instance, and the sense of *gratitude* [Italics added; Gk. *euchariston*] . . . we should be giving thanks to God for those things for which we ought to give Him thanks.'

[217] May be also 'the law of God' in Rom 7:22, according to Udo Schnelle, *The Human Condition* (Minneapolis: Fortress, 1996), 71.

[218] Plutarch, E Delph. 20, cited in Udo Schnelle, *Theology of the New Testament*, trans. M. E. Boring (Grand Rapids: Baker, 2007), 218. According to Schnelle, "There were two sources of the knowledge of God: (1) the idea of deity implanted in the human consciousness in view of the majesty of the cosmos [Mesographic

revelation?], and (2) the traditional images of God conveyed in the old myths and customs." This second 'source' is condemned in Rom. 1:18-32; it is nothing but an imaginative corruption of the first. The point is conceded even by a First Century pagan (Pliny, *Nat. Hist.* 2.26-27) who excoriates those "worshiping ghosts and making a god of one who has already ceased to be even a man." Idem, *Theology of the New Testament*, 226.

[219] 2 Esdras 7:72 (RSV) http://quod.lib.umich.edu/cgi/r/rsv/rsv-idx?type=DIV1&byte=3652195.

[220] W. A. VanGemeren, "The Law is the Perfection of Righteousness in Jesus Christ: A Reformed Perspective," in *The Law, The Gospel, and the Modern Christian: Five Views*, ed. Greg L. Bahnsen et al. (Grand Rapids: Zondervan, 2007), 21. We agree withVanGemeren although we express some reservation about the virtual immutability of the law.

[221] C. L. Blomberg and Mariam J. Kamell, *James: Exegetical Commentary on the New Testament* (Grand Rapids: Zondervan, 2008), 91-92.

[222] I.e., "the Faith of Jesus"?

[223] Geza Vermes, *The Complete Dead Sea Scrolls in English* (London: Penguin, 1997), 391-392. Italics added; cf. also the following with its NT fulfilment: "He who liberates the captives, restores sight to the blind, straightens the b[ent] . . . For He will heal the wounded, and revive the dead and bring good news to the poor." The "holy ones" in Hebrew could also be construed as singular (the Holy One) as in Prov. 9:10; taken this way the reference is to YHWH and not primarily to the saints.

[224] Conzelmann's comment on 15:20 to the effect that "The intention of the [apostolic] decree is not to retain the Law as valid, not even symbolically or 'in principle'" may be too strong; *Acts*, 118. For a more nuanced approach, see Justin Taylor, "The Jerusalem Decrees (Acts 15.20,29 and 21.25) and the Incident at Antioch," 47 (July 2001): 372-380.

[225] Borrowed from mesographos "drawn [or written] in the middle [heart?]" (H. Liddell and R. Scott, *An Intermediate Greek-English Lexicon* [Oxford: Clarendon 1997], 500).

[226] Believers today, like Luke and Paul, should see themselves as under law to Christ (1 Cor. 9:21b; D.A. Carson, "Mystery and Fulfilment: Toward a More Comprehensive Paradigm of Paul's Understanding of the Old and the New," in *Justification and Variegated Nomism: The Paradoxes of Paul*, ed. Mark A. Seifrid et al. [Grand Rapids: Baker, 2004], 402); their directives (1 Cor. 9:19b) are to be found here, minus the command to be circumcised (Acts 15; 1 Cor. 9:19a)—and a whole lot more. It would appear that Paul mentions all three ethical codes in Romans (the Mesographic for the Gentiles in Rom. 1:32— They know God's decree "; The Mosaic for the Jews— Rom. 2:12—"[A]ll who have sinned under the law will be judged by the law," cf. 3:1-2; and the Messianic for Christians in Rom. 6:17— "But thanks be to God that you, having once been slaves of sin, have become obedient from the heart to the form of teaching to which you were entrusted" (NRSV; italics mine. See also Isa 42:4b).

[227] See Appendix 6

[228] Or even to circumcise one's son for that matter; or somebody else's (Acts) as a missionary strategy. The point is none of these Mosaic precepts or principles should attain the status of categorical imperatives; they are relativized (not abolished) by the coming of Messiah and are therefore without salvific value, absolutely.

[229] "BDAG 780 s.v. παροξυσμός 2 has *"sharp disagreement"* here; L&N 33.451 has "sharp argument, sharp difference of opinion" (NET notes); interestingly, after this incident Paul will use this term (παροξυσμός) in 1 Cor 13 to describe what love is not. S. Lewis Johnson in his commentary on First Corinthians points out that the KJV translation "not easily provoked" has no basis in the Greek text. In other words, παροξυσμός has no qualifier. If the addition of "easily" is misleading, there is at least one modern translation that has followed the AV in this error.

[230] Seen here as the outworking of God's plan (26:30-32; cf. 2:23), about which Luke has much to say (e.g., 27:21-25; see also D.G. Peterson, *The Acts of the Apostles* [Grand Rapids: Eerdmans, 2009], 29-32, and J T Squires, 'The Plan of God,' in *Witness to the Gospel: The Theology of Acts*, ed. I H Marshall and D Peterson (Grand Rapids: Eerdmans, 1998), 19-37.

CHAPTER 16

1- 15 WITH THE CONFLICT AND the council out of the way, Luke returns to the itinerary of first-century Christian missionary engagement. The council, however, reminds the reader that such engagement needs the kind of theological reflection that will ensure such engagement's integrity vis-à-vis the missionary context and its proper canonical alignment. So, in this chapter, Paul is once again on the move, this time with a new colleague. His next challenge, though not overtly theological as the council, is not without doctrinal and inter-personal import.

Two of the NT books bear the name Timothy; here we are introduced to the lad himself—the child of a mixed marriage (1-2). He must have been a pious and brave lad to agree to circumcision long past eight days old. But knowing his own background in Jewry, Paul the delegate of Christ will do anything to reach out to his fellowmen (v 3; cf. Rom 9:1-3; 10:1-3; 11:1; 1 Cor 9:19-21).

Having circumcised Timothy, they passed on the decisions of the Jerusalem council for Gentile churches (4); whether there is a causal relationship between the growth of the assemblies and the events of the previous chapter or not, Luke wants us to know that despite pressure of one kind or the other churches can still experience genuine progress in the faith (5). The Spirit's prohibition of the following couple of verses (6-7) does not negate this, for the steps (as well as the stops!) of good men are ordered by the Lord.[231]

Following the prohibition of verse 7 we have a night vision[232] in the verses immediately following. It was this divine direction that eventually introduced the gospel into Europe (8-9). The missioners (including Dr Luke) finally settled in Philippi where the church which was to become a favourite of Paul was birthed (10-15).[233]

The first convert (through open-heart surgery) was a godly woman[234] who regularly participated in a riverside[235] prayer meeting (13-14). It was her house (with husband, children and servants?) that—in all probability—later hosted the people of God (including the convert of vv 16-34?) on a Sunday[236] (15).

16-34 The book of Acts turns out to be a series of setbacks[237] and successes; the setback on this occasion comes from a demon possessed lass. Having arrived in Philippi, the chief city of Macedonia, the team's first converts, as we have seen above, were Lydia and members of her household. In the case of Lydia, one senses the heart of God in his eagerness to reach the heart of humanity (14).

If there is success with Lydia, there is trouble ahead with this other female (16). In contrast to Lydia, this one appears willing to help the evangelists announce the way (17). Both Bruce and more recently Schnabel express

CHAPTER 16

doubts concerning this superficial understanding of the girl's assistance. Bruce, for instance, suggests the following translation: "a way of salvation."[238]

Wallace simply labels the construction debatable.[239] Certainly the evangelistic team was not amused with such promotion; eventually, the team was incarcerated for voicing their concern in the form of an exorcism (18-24).

> But at midnight Paul and Silas were praying and singing hymns to God, and the prisoners were listening to them. 26 Suddenly there was a great earthquake, so that the foundations of the prison were shaken; and immediately all the doors were opened and everyone's chains were loosed. 27 And the keeper of the prison, awaking from sleep and seeing the prison doors open, supposing the prisoners had fled, drew his sword and was about to kill himself. 28 But Paul called with a loud voice, saying, "Do yourself no harm, for we are all here." 29 Then he called for a light, ran in, and fell down trembling before Paul and Silas. 30 And he brought them out and said, "Sirs, what must I do to be saved?" 31 So they said, "Believe on the Lord Jesus Christ, and you will be saved, you and your household."

Verse 25 is a surprising response on the part of Paul and Silas. The fact that the prisoners heard, most likely for the first time a redemption song, may explain the jailer's question in verse 30, after the divine intervention (26-29). He too was a prisoner of sorts; his eyes and those of his family were opened that night (31-34).

35-40 With the jailer released from his spiritual darkness, it was Silas and Paul's turn to be free from their unjust incarceration (35-39). Before their departure they received much comfort from the fellowship of the new Macedonian believers (40).

---

[231] In verses 6 and 7 the willing witnesses are hindered from serving in the province of Asia and Bythinnia but allowed to pass through "the region of Phrygia and Galatia," (v. 6) having passed by Mysia on their way to Troas (v. 8).

[232] It is said that visions normally come in the day (cf. Paul and Peter in chapters 9-10) and dreams by night; but what about people like myself who day-dream?

[233] In verse 10 "called" is also used not to denote an initial summon to missionary engagement but further guidance. The verse also implies that visions and dreams must be interpreted correctly.

[234] A friend of mine observed that in the vision Paul saw a man but his first convert was of the opposite sex. Would he have responded the same way if he had seen a woman? God always knows best.

[235] Lydia was very likely baptized here.

[236] On this see Appendix 6.

[237] One wonders if Paul and Silas entertained any doubt concerning their mission (especially the former whose 'ungrateful' behaviour toward Barnabas, the brother who was instrumental in introducing him to the fledgling Messianic community). If they had any misgivings concerning the viability of their missionary enterprise, it was soon removed by that Macedonian vision that clarified their mission, while at the same helping them to understand the perceived setbacks.

[238] F.F. Bruce, *Acts*, 316.

[239] Daniel B. Wallace, Greek Grammar Beyond the Basics: An Exegetical Syntax of the New Testament (Grand Rapids: Zondervan, 1996), 101.

CHAPTER 17

1-12 THE NEXT EUROPEAN STOP is in "Thessalonica where there was a synagogue of the Jews." There Paul expounded the Jewish sacred writings for three weeks with much success (1-4). But as we have seen before there is trouble on the horizon soon after a new set of people experience human flourishing as God intends it (5-9).[240] This new wave of pressure from unbelievers prompts the believers to act by sending Paul and his companion to Berea.

In 1997 I was privileged to attend an international conference in Little Rock, Arkansas; there I met at brother from Greece. I asked him where in Greece he lived and he responded, "Thessaloniki—well not quite; a nearby town called Berea". I recall borrowing his Bible for the night; 'twas all Greek to me!' The Bereans of Paul's day were careful to examine everything the fugitive apostle proclaimed from the Greek Bible of the time.[241]

Both the expository interpretation of Paul and the thorough investigation of the noble Bereans resulted in a rich harvest of souls (10-12). This experience must have had a lasting effect on Paul and explains in part his counsel to the Thessalonians (1 Thess. 5:19-22; especially v 21). But before Paul wrote he had to beat another hasty retreat (13-14).

15-34   He is now in the famous Greek city awaiting two of his colleagues; but he is ill-at-ease. To every pious Jew or Christian—yesterday and today—the most heinous category of sins is that of idolatry (cf. Exodus 20: 1-3). That is what piqued Paul the most.

So he did something about it (15-17). Just when he could bear it no longer some philosophers of Epicurean and Stoic persuasion challenged him on his talk about one Jesus and related resurrection matters. They wanted to hear more (18-21). We may paraphrase a part of Luke's account as follows:

> Then Paul stands in the midst of Mars' Hill and says, "Men of Athens, I perceive that in every respect you are quite religious; for as I passed by and observed your devotedness, I found an altar with this inscription: 'To the Unknown God'. Well, he whom you worship unknowingly I now declare to you. It is this God who created the universe and everything in it.
>
> Since he is Lord of Heaven and earth, he does not dwell in man-made temples. Neither is he in need of anything from humanity, because he is the Giver of all things, including life and breath. Moreover, he made of one blood all nations to dwell on the earth, and has determined the times appointed, and the boundaries of their sojourn. He did this so that all peoples should seek the Lord, if perchance they might sense his presence

and find him, because he is not far from any one of us. For in him we live, and move, and exist; as also certain of your own poets have said, 'For we are also his offspring.'

Since we are the offspring of God, we should not think that the supreme Deity is like gold or silver or stone, the artistic expressions of any one's imagination. Let it be known that God overlooked such times of this ignorance, and now summons all to repentance. In fact, he has appointed a Day in which he will bring the world into righteous judgment by an appointed Person, whom he raised from the dead as proof (22-31).

The majority of the Athenians could not stomach any talk of a resurrection, given the philosophy of the day. However, a few did respond positively, both women and men: Praise the Lord! (32-34)

Summary

In Thessalonica for over two weeks, Paul "reasoned with them from the Scriptures, explaining and proving that the Christ had to suffer and rise from the dead" (3). The results of Paul's exposition of the Scriptures were encouraging; willing hearts—women and men—responded positively (4). Others responded negatively (vv 5-10). The retreat of the missionaries, Paul and Silas, to Berea reminds one of the dominical counsel of Matt 10:23.

The Bereans, Luke informs us, appear to be model disciples from the get go (11-12), but just as it was in Thessalonica, opposition came from some adherents of

Judaism. This resulted in a temporary separation of the team with the apostle Paul ending up in Athens. Again, Paul's ministry began in the synagogue, but it was not restricted there (18).

His presence in the Greek capital afforded Paul the opportunity to witness to two of the most prominent philosophical groups of the day: The Epicureans and the Stoics. Keener's comment on this episode is apropos: "If Paul is like a new Socrates . . ., then he, rather than the novelty-seeking Athenians (21), stands in continuity with the true philosophic tradition."[242] If philosophy is seen (broadly speaking) as a way of life, Paul was completely sold out to the Way, the Truth and the Life, and was thoroughly convinced that others should be also (cf. Rom. 1:1-3).

---

[240] In v 6 God's servants are accused thus: "These who have turned the world upside down have come here too" (NKJV). The irony is that the movement was doing the opposite; it still does by the grace of God.

[241] Assuming here that both the preacher and his audience had access to the AV of the day: the LXX.

[242] Keener, *Acts*, 2:625.

CHAPTER 18

THE ABOVE CONVICTION takes the apostle to Achaia (18:1-27), to Ephesus (chaps 19-20), back to Jerusalem (chapts 21-26), and finally to Rome itself—all along through much trial and tribulation. In his own words, he has:

> been in prison more frequently, been flogged more severely, and been exposed to death again and again.[24] Five times I received from the Jews the forty lashes minus one.[25] Three times I was beaten with rods, once I was pelted with stones, three times I was shipwrecked, I spent a night and a day in the open sea,[26] I have been constantly on the move. I have been in danger from rivers, in danger from bandits, in danger from my fellow Jews, in danger from Gentiles; in danger in the city, in danger in the country, in danger at sea; and in danger from false believers.[27] I have labored and toiled and have often gone without sleep; I have known hunger and thirst and have often gone without food; I have been cold and naked.[28] Besides everything else, I

face daily the pressure of my concern for all the churches.²⁹ Who is weak, and I do not feel weak? Who is led into sin, and I do not inwardly burn? (2 Cor 11: 23-28).

2-17 Whether Paul is in Athens, Jerusalem or Rome, whether incarcerated or not, like his Master, his major concern is for people, especially the Messianic community and its potential membership. This is also borne out by his visit to Corinth (1). There he finds a couple of kindred spirit (2-3).

But Priscilla and her husband were not the only like-minded companions of Paul in Corinth; Silas, his original partner on the second missionary journey, and Timothy also joined him. This enabled Paul to give himself more fully to the task of teaching and evangelism in the synagogue and elsewhere (4-6).

After his extended synagogue ministry in Corinth was cut short, Paul was fortunate to receive hospitality from a God-fearing Gentile. Better still, news came that "Crispus, the leader of the synagogue, and his entire household believed in the Lord and were baptized—as were many others in Corinth"! (7-8 TLB).

Paul and the other members of the team were no doubt elated over this turn of events. If the Corinthian hospitality and the salvation of the Crispus' household were not enough good news for the team, the blessed Lord himself communicated with the team leader and in so doing calmed his fears, and shared with him that wicked Corinth would have an assembly of genuine believers in short order (9-11).

CHAPTER 18

So what's new? There is opposition just around the corner from Paul's own people once again. This time around, though, the opposition was chastened by a new governor of the region. The resulting trial of the missionary was adjourned prematurely, leaving the accusers quite angry. What happened next is a case of, what they say in Jamaica, *caa ketch Quaku yu ketch im shut*,[243] for as Crispus was saved from the wrath of God, his successor was not spared the wrath of man (12-17).

After yet another threat on his life the apostle to the Gentiles still lingers awhile in Corinth. Why? It is highly likely that the vision he received earlier imparted much courage, immediately after his initial fear (cf. 2 Tim 1:7)—and after all, God's servant is immortal until the Messiah, the One who holds the keys of death, is ready for her or him.[244]

As he makes his way back to his sending assembly in Syria, he is accompanied by his new friends Priscilla[245] and Aquila; he also takes time out to get a haircut (18).[246] So when Paul and his companions Silas, Luke, and the married couple, arrived at Ephesus by boat, he went alone to the Jewish synagogue to discuss certain matters (relating to the vow?) and also made plans to return *Deo volente*.[247]

His next stop is in the Holy Land, the port of Caesarea to be exact. The Paul of Acts was never a busybody. But he was certainly busy! At one moment he is in Jerusalem. Then he is miles away to the north (Antioch). Next thing you know he is in the familiar territory of Asia Minor (Turkey; vv 18-23). Shortly after, he meets a Bible teacher that goes by the name of Apollos. This servant appears to be an African native of Jewish extraction who is familiar with the ministry of the greatest human being under the Old Covenant (Matt 11:11).

Apollos was an orator and shared what he knows with much enthusiasm. But his preaching lacked depth, since he was unaware of the fact that the One to whom John the Baptizer (Dipper)[248] pointed was glorified years ago. Fortunately for Apollos the dynamic team of Priscilla and Aquila was on hand to set him straight concerning the Way (24-26). The exemplary couple caught up with him just in time, because he is heading for Greece. There he will make a name for himself (27-28) and become the *de facto* leader of a significant portion of the church at Corinth (1 Cor. 3:4).

---

[243] Jean Lee ('Men and the Family,' 65-66, https://biblicalstudies.org.uk/pdf/cjet/11_040.pdf. The phrase also helps to explain Jamaica's high murder rate; every act of murder is really rage against the out-of-reach Creator (Gen 9; cf. James 3).

[244] Moreover, if the Narrator is seen as a screen writer and the book of Acts the actual movie, then the stars (Peter in 1-12; Paul in the remaining chapters) cannot die.

[245] On female leadership in the NT see chapter 10 of *Romans in Context* (Eugene, OR: RP, 2011), as well as Appendix 9.

[246] He was in all likelihood fulfilling a Nazarite vow. At first I thought he Dread!

[247] See Appendix 4.

[248] ***Josephus is worth hearing on this matter:***

> Now some of the Jews thought the destruction of Herod's army came from God, and was just punishment for what he did against John called the Baptist [the dipper]. For Herod had him killed, although he was a good man and had urged

CHAPTER 18

the Jews to exert themselves to virtue, both as to justice toward one another and reverence towards God, and having done so join together in washing. For immersion in water, it was clear to him, could not be used for the forgiveness of sins, but as a sanctification of the body, and only if the soul was already thoroughly purified by right actions. And when others massed about him, for they were very greatly moved by his words, Herod, who feared that such strong influence over the people might carry to a revolt -- for they seemed ready to do anything he should advise -- believed it much better to move now than later have it raise a rebellion and engage him in actions he would regret. And so John, out of Herod's suspiciousness, was sent in chains to Machaerus, the fort previously mentioned, and there put to death; but it was the opinion of the Jews that out of retribution for John God willed the destruction of the army so as to afflict Herod." (Emphasis added). Antiquities 18.5.*2 116-119.*
http://www.josephus.org/JohnTBaptist.htm#Purification

CHAPTER 19

1-7 APOLLOS LEFT EPHESUS to go to Corinth (18:24). Just around that time Paul arrives in Ephesus, and by the time he leaves he will plant a church in that city—a church that will become the most fortunate, judging from the quality ministry it will receive in the first century. For example, by the end of the century it received seven letters from God's choicest servants: Ephesians, First and Second Timothy, First, Second, and Third John, and finally, Revelation 2:1-7.

Interestingly, all of these letters in one way or the other deal with the supreme virtue of love as the driving force behind the Christian life and ministry. The first (Ephesians 6:24) provides special incentive for those who take what we may call vertical love seriously, and the last—some twenty five years after—shows how busy we can become, doing the Lord's work without the proper motivation (cf. 2 Cor 5:14) that comes from the Spirit (Ephesians 5:18; cf Gal 5:15-23).

Sadly, the Holy Spirit can be resident (John 14:15-16) but not president of our lives. Paul's ministry this time around gives him a wonderful opportunity to introduce the Spirit to a group of religious adherents, who, like Apollos in the earlier days, just knew about John's ministry (1-7; cf. Rom 8:9).[249]

8-20 Verses 8-10 give us a brief account of the founding of the Ephesian Church, with the aforementioned twelve disciples as foundation members:

> Then Paul went to the synagogue and preached boldly each Sabbath day[b] for three, telling what he believed and why,* and persuading many to believe in Jesus. ⁹ But some rejected his message and publicly spoke against Christ, so he left, refusing to preach to them again. Pulling out the believers, he began a separate meeting at the lecture hall of Tyrannus and preached there daily. ¹⁰ This went on for the next two years, so that everyone in the Turkish province of Asia Minor—both Jews and Greeks—heard the Lord's message (NLT).

The ministry of Paul over the three-year period closely resembles that of his Lord and Master in terms of its power impact on the city (11-12). It attracts attention (what else is new!) from the kingdom of darkness and eventually ends in triumph for the kingdom of Light (13-20).[250]

We suggested earlier that the apostle's experience in Berea influenced his penning of 1 Thessalonians 5:21. We further suggest that the power encounters in the city led Paul to write these sobering words (Ephesians 6:10-20):

CHAPTER 19

God is strong, and he wants you strong. So take everything the Master has set out for you, well-made weapons of the best materials. And put them to use so you will be able to stand up to everything the Devil throws your way. This is no afternoon athletic contest that we'll walk away from and forget about in a couple of hours. This is for keeps, a life-or-death fight to the finish against the Devil and all his angels. [13-18] Be prepared. You're up against far more than you can handle on your own. Take all the help you can get, every weapon God has issued, so that when it's all over but the shouting you'll still be on your feet. Truth, righteousness, peace, faith, and salvation are more than words. Learn how to apply them.

You'll need them throughout your life. God's Word is an indispensable weapon. In the same way, prayer is essential in this ongoing warfare. Pray hard and long. Pray for your brothers and sisters. Keep your eyes open. Keep each other's spirits up so that no one falls behind or drops out. [19-20] And don't forget to pray for me. Pray that I'll know what to say and have the courage to say it at the right time, telling the mystery to one and all, the Message that I, jailbird preacher that I am, am responsible for getting out (The Message).

21-41 Well over two years in one place for Paul is a long time. He will stay longer, although the Spirit is leading him elsewhere. It appears that Philippi, Thessalonica, and Athens are still on his mind.

Definitely Jerusalem and Rome are on the radar. Division of labour demands at this time that his colleagues share the burden (21-22). Ephesus will receive more of Luke's attention for the reason that it illustrates how the ideals of the Gospel can clash with the greed of big business partners who care not about the light of kingdom (23-41; cf. Mark 5).

The temple of Diana was at that time one of the seven wonders of the ancient world.[251] When Paul eventually wrote his famous letter to the Ephesian believers, he reminded them that it is they that constitute God's masterpiece, not that of Diana or Artemis (Eph 2:10).

---

[249] So far in the book of Acts we have seen people tarrying for the Spirit (1:5), identifying themselves with the name of Jesus to receive the Spirit (2:38), having hands laid on them for the Spirit's anointing (8 and 9), in chapter 11 people are baptized by the Spirit before the conclusion of the sermon. Here it is laying on of hands once more, accompanied with tongues and prophecy. Which of these experiences is normative today? There is no definitive answer from Dr Luke. Another question begs itself: What is the normative (if any) accompanying sign(s) of the Spirit's initial presence in the believer—speaking in tongues, prophesying, sound of a hurricane, laying on of hands, prayer, cloven tongues of fire? Only one thing seems certain (according to Luke travelling companion); without the indwelling Spirit in my life I don't belong to Christ (Eph 1:13-14; Rom 5:5; 8:9).

[250] Note especially vv 18-19: "Many of the believers who had been practicing black magic confessed their deeds and brought their incantation books and charms and burned them at a public bonfire. (Someone estimated the value of the books at $10,000 . . . approximately £3,500). This indicates how deeply the whole area was stirred by God's message." NLT.

[251] Antipater of Sidon was reported to have said: "I have seen the . . . Hanging Gardens of ancient Babylon, the statue of Olympian Zeus, the Colossus of Rhodes, the mighty work of the high Pyramids and the tomb of Mausoulos. But when I saw the temple of Ephesus rising to the clouds, all these wonders were put in the shade." http://www.unmuseum.org/ephesus.htm. See also ABD.

CHAPTER 20

1-6 **THESE VERSES NOTE** the sequel of the events of the previous chapter by setting out the itinerary and obstacles of the missionaries:

> After the uproar died down, Paul called together the believers and with words of encouragement said good-bye to them. Then he left and went on to Macedonia. ² He went through those regions and encouraged the people with many messages. Then he came to Achaia, ³ where he stayed three months. He was getting ready to go to Syria when he discovered that there were Jews plotting against him; so he decided to go back through Macedonia. ⁴ Sopater son of Pyrrhus, from Berea, went with him; so did Aristarchus and Secundus, from Thessalonica; Gaius, from Derbe; Tychicus and Trophimus, from the province of Asia; and Timothy. ⁵ They went ahead and waited for us in Troas. ⁶ We sailed from Philippi after the Festival of Unleavened Bread, and five days later we

joined them in Troas, where we spent a week (Good News Bible).

7-16 Again the apostle Paul is highlighted in these verses in which we get a glimpse of the Sunday worship[252] of the early believers outside of Palestine. This time around it is a valedictory service in the evening that ended in tragedy and triumph—and more travelling. Verse 16 mentions the day of Pentecost for the final time in this book. The first was extraordinary; this one was not. We recall that

The Spirit came on the Jewish feast of Pentecost, a time when representatives from different nations and Jews from the diaspora converge on Jerusalem for business, pleasure, and religion. What Luke calls the Day of Pentecost ... was one of the earliest of the three major feasts.... As a means of legitimizing their already sacred calendar, Jewish tradition has it that God also gave the Torah (the law) to Israel on the Day of Pentecost, fifty days after Passover, thus adding double significance to the feast.[253]

So why was Paul rushing to celebrate Pentecost? Certainly, he must have heard of what happened on the earlier Pentecost recorded in chapter 2, even before he became a Christian. Possibly his haste was motivated by his missionary strategy outlined in 1 Corinthians 9. We should not be surprised either if he was hoping to reap another harvest of souls as Peter did on that very special occasion--and if he believed the Jewish tradition cited above, he would have been only too eager to teach new believers about the

CHAPTER 20

Messianic law that was formerly introduced as in Acts 2:42a (cf. our notes above on chapter 15).

17-36 Paul's next discourse is introduced thus:

> And from Miletus he sent to Ephesus, and called the elders of the church. And when they were come to him, he said unto them, Ye know, from the first day that I came into Asia, after what manner I have been with you at all seasons, serving the Lord with all humility of mind, and with many tears, and temptations, which befell me by the lying in wait of the Jews: and how I kept back nothing that was profitable to you, but have shewed you, and have taught you publicly, and from house to house...Wherefore I take you to record this day, that I am pure from the blood of all men. For I have not shunned to declare unto all the counsel of God." (Acts 20:17-20, 26-27).

Two verses are worthy of serious consideration: verses 20 and 27. The latter is an expansion of the former. Once again, we turn to Acts 20:17-35. What Paul did among the early converts at Ephesus was not accidental. He consciously stressed certain traits and habits, because he wanted his spiritual children to follow suit.

If the Ephesian elders had missed this point, the apostle is at pains here to put the issue beyond doubt. He wanted to underscore such virtues as humility, patience (v. 14), longsuffering, boldness (v. 20, 21, 22, 23, 24) faithfulness (26, 27) and watchfulness (v. 28-31). He was particularly desirous of imparting to his converts in general and leaders in particular a meaningful work ethic.

I have coveted no man's silver, or gold, or apparel. Yea, ye yourselves know that these hands have ministered unto my necessities and to them that were with me. I have shewed you all things, how that so labouring ye ought to support the weak, and to remember the words of the Lord Jesus, how he said, It is more blessed to give than to receive (20:33-35).

This is confirmed by his reference to this same kind of ethic in Ephesians 4:28, and his use of the word 'labour' on both occasions.

If one does not understand the apostle, his anxiety to have people follow his pattern of life seems to border almost on egotism. Indeed, an enumeration of the number of personal references in Acts 20 would definitely convince some of his conceit. But statistics in this case does not give a true picture of the man. Living an exemplary life was at the root of his strategy to train leaders.

Twice Paul urged the Philippians to take his lifestyle seriously (Phil. 3:17; 4:9). According to Lofthouse, this apostle is "the most self-conscious of all writers of the New Testament".[254] A perusal of his letters and of this chapter in particular (with at least fourteen self-references) seems to justify this claim. If John Stott is nervous about dominical I-locutions,[255] he seems to be more comfortable with similar statements by Paul.

Commenting on verses 22-27, he writes: "In this section Luke replaces the 'you know . . . you know . . . of the previous paragraph with I know (23)... I know (23) . . ., I know (29) . . .' For he turns from the past which they knew, to the future".[256] These I-sayings highlighted by

CHAPTER 20

Stott may be regarded as personal reflections with a definite paradigmatic design, because the Pauline pronouns, as elsewhere, "are not narrowly autobiographical. He presents his own perspective as exemplary for all believers."[257]

Interestingly, NT scholars are more enamoured with the 'We' passages, and as far as I can see, very little attention is given to the I-declarations in Acts. Rasta hermeneutics has the potential of correcting that. We will now examine the other I-statements in Luke's report of the Miletus meeting.

The declarations within this speech were uttered in roughly the same region of Caesar's "I came, I saw, I conquered."[258] They somewhat remind one of a later Lord who once came, saw, conquered—and one of whose dying words was actually an I-declaration ("I thirst!"), allowing the Ephesian elders to later drink of the water of life. The temple of Artemis, as we have pointed out before, was probably well known to these elders, as one of the seven wonders of the ancient world.

Little did those elders know that they became a part of the only institution—a permanent institution of sheer divine artistry (Eph. 2:8-10)—that will integrally constitute the new universe,[259] purchased with blood divine ("Keep watch over yourselves, and all the flock over whom the Holy Spirit has appointed you supervisors, to shepherd God's church that He purchased with the blood of His own"[Son][260] v. 28).[261] It is in this light that we should understand the other Pauline statement:

The 'I' of Pastoral Commitment (31)

The 'I' of Prayerful Commendation (32)

The 'I' of Personal Conviction (33-34)

The 'I': The Paradigmatic Christ (35)

This final declaration is climactic, precisely because it is Christocentric. It echoes in a very definite way the programmatic declaration of Luke 4 whose structure, according David Pao, looks like this:

A. synagogue (16a)
B. Jesus standing (16b)
C. Jesus given the scroll (17a)
   D Jesus' reading from Isaiah (18-19)
C'. Jesus giving back the scroll (20a)
B'. Jesus sitting (20b)
A'. synagogue (20c)[262]

A comparison of the two discourses, that is, of Acts 20:35 and the longer one in the Gospel, helps the reader to appreciate better what Luke means by the 'weak' and the 'poor'—all the marginalized, disenfranchised, imprisoned—in a word—the enslaved. The whole discourse of Acts is dedicated to fleshing out these themes first enunciated in the Third Gospel.

But there is a question we need to ask at this juncture: Why did Luke not include the dominical saying of verse

CHAPTER 20

28 in his first volume? It seems that he, via the route of inter-textuality, has done so to tighten the connection between the Messiah and the apostle to the Gentiles, similar to what is done elsewhere.

For example, in 13:47 there is also an important echo of Luke 2:32, where similar language is used of Jesus. The Mission of the Servant is undertaken both by Jesus (cf. 26:23) and, to a far lesser extent, Paul, who with much difficulty managed to tear himself away from his beloved brethren (36).

---

[252] Appendix 6.
[253] N S Murrell, "Hermeneutics as Interpretation, Part 2," *CJET* 3 (1999), 58
[254] Lofthouse 1952, 241
[255] It appears that Stott (2003, 36) finds this Johannine phenomenon a trifle suspicious: "This prominence of the personal pronoun ("I- I- I- . . .") is very disturbing, especially in one who declared humility to be the pre-eminent virtue."
[256] *The Spirit, the Church and the World* (Downers Gove, IL: IVP, 1990), 325.
[257] D.J. Moo, *Galatians* (Grand Rapids: Baker, 2013), 395.
[258] Suetonius.
[259] On this, see Middleton, *New Heavens*.
[260] The 'Word' that became flesh (John 1:14) was a theological and redemptive necessity; the Son of God had to become human in order to die as the spotless Lamb of God (John 1:29). And he had to retain his divinity (John 1:1c), in order to give global and eternal value to his sacrifice. If Jesus were a sinner, he could only have died for his own sins (Rom 6:23a); if he were only a perfect human, he could only have died for one other person—most likely for someone in the Caribbean (conventional substitution)! But being the unique (monogenēs) member of the God-head, the only one to have taken on permanent human status, his death has value for all humanity, and his resurrection by the Spirit (Rom 1:1-4), the Father (Rom 6:4), and the Son of Man (John 2:19) makes available a right relationship with God (Rom 4:25). "'Tis mystery all!"

[261] Note the Trinitarian construction in our translation; Peterson, 568, following Barrett, sees this verse as the theological and practical centre of the speech, laying bare the apostle's intention to impress upon the elders the gravity of their calling (practical dimension), as well as the paramount importance of the atonement (theological dimension; cf. Lk 18:31-34; 24: 13-49) as a basis for their continued commitment and ministry.

[262] David Pao, *Acts*, 71-71.

CHAPTER 21

THROUGHOUT THEIR HISTORY the Jews never had any outstanding maritime experience like that of their neighbors to the north, such as Tyre.[263] Yes, there is the famous story of Jonah, that troublesome passenger, who wished he had a vessel that could travel the speed of light[264] (my interpretation of the "wings of the morn"). In his desperation he also thought of self-propulsion ("the wings of a dove"). He is probably the first to travel in a submarine[265] (without having a whale of a time at that!). Then there is the Ultimate Master of the sea who walked on it,[266] the One of whom Jonah served as a type. He is the same One who made a Rock (i.e., Peter/Cephas) walk on water. As was said before, the Book of Acts may be biographically delineated as follows: Peter (1-12), Paul (13-28).

Most, if not all, of Peter's encounter with the water comes in the Gospels, including the walking miracle. All of Paul's in Acts are related to his missionary journeys and trip to the eternal city.[267] In chapters 21 to the end of the book Paul's travelling companion chronicles many of these voyages. For example:

> When we had parted from them and set sail, we came by a straight course to Cos, and the next day to Rhodes, and from there to Patara. [a] ² When we found a ship bound for Phoenicia, we went on board and set sail. ³ We came in sight of Cyprus; and leaving it on our left, we sailed to Syria and landed at Tyre, because the ship was to unload its cargo there. ⁴ We looked up the disciples and stayed there for seven days. Through the Spirit they told Paul not to go on to Jerusalem. ⁵ When our days there were ended, we left and proceeded on our journey; and all of them, with wives and children, escorted us outside the city. There we knelt down on the beach and prayed ⁶ and said farewell to one another. Then we went on board the ship, and they returned home.⁷ When we had finished the voyage from Tyre, we arrived at Ptolemais; and we greeted the believers and stayed with them for one day (RSV).

8-26 The team finally arrives in Caesarea and visits Philip the evangelist, whose daughters are prophetesses.[268] While there the same prophet who had made his way to the north in chapter 11 does something similar on this occasion. The famine he had predicted earlier was evidently over, but this time the bad news is for the team leader, Paul. His dramatic message to the apostle is reminiscent of those of Ezekiel. Agabus's prophecy is basically a forewarning and forearming communiqué, but the other members of the team (and the believers present) did not see it that way (8-12).

CHAPTER 21

> [13] Then Paul answered, "What are you doing, weeping and breaking my heart? For I am ready not only to be bound but even to die in Jerusalem for the name of the Lord Jesus." [14] Since he would not be persuaded, we remained silent except to say,[269] "The Lord's will be done."[15] After these days we got ready and started to go up to Jerusalem. [16] Some of the disciples from Caesarea also came along and brought us to the house of Mnason of Cyprus, an early disciple, with whom we were to stay (RSV).

So, Paul finally reaches the Holy City once again, despite warnings associated with the Spirit of God. Was he on those occasions disobedient to the voice of God, or was he putting into practice his own wise counsel (1 Thess. 5:21)? The latter is most surely the case. A warm welcome awaits him, and his presence becomes the catalyst to give God praise (17-20a). But how good was Paul in accepting the counsel of others? (20b-26).

27-40 The apostle wisely did as he was told by the Jews in Jerusalem but some Jews from the Diaspora, who were apparently envious of his success among the Gentiles, tracked him down with murderous intent. The servant is not greater than the Master (cf. John 8).

> [27] When the seven days were almost completed, the Jews from Asia, who had seen him in the temple, stirred up the whole crowd. They seized him, [28] shouting, "Fellow Israelites, help! This is the man who is teaching everyone everywhere against our people, our law, and this place; more than that, he has actually brought

ACTS

Greeks into the temple and has defiled this holy place." ²⁹ For they had previously seen Trophimus the Ephesian with him in the city, and they supposed that Paul had brought him into the temple. ³⁰
Then all the city was aroused, and the people rushed together. They seized Paul and dragged him out of the temple, and immediately the doors were shut. ³¹ While they were trying to kill him, word came to the tribune of the cohort that all Jerusalem was in an uproar. ³² Immediately he took soldiers and centurions and ran down to them.
When they saw the tribune and the soldiers, they stopped beating Paul. ³³ Then the tribune came, arrested him, and ordered him to be bound with two chains; he inquired who he was and what he had done. ³⁴ Some in the crowd shouted one thing, some another; and as he could not learn the facts because of the uproar, he ordered him to be brought into the barracks. ³⁵ When Paul[f] came to the steps, the violence of the mob was so great that he had to be carried by the soldiers. ³⁶ The crowd that followed kept shouting, "Away with him!" (RSV)

The closing verses of this chapter demonstrate without the shadow of a doubt that Paul's love for his people is far greater than his love for his own life (Rom 9), and his commitment to the defence of the gospel (whether in an African,²⁷⁰ Hellenistic or Hebrew tongue) is second to none. His apologetic response will await the following chapter. Enjoy the cliff hanger.²⁷¹

---

²⁶³ But see 2 Kings 8.

CHAPTER 21

[264] Psalm 139:9.

[265] Literal meaning: below sea level; not to be confused with my grades in school—below 'C' level.

[266] John 6:16-21.

[267] What Peter had over Paul was the experience of walking on a lake; what Paul had over him was a flight to heaven.

[268] see Beverley Roberts Gaventa, "Whatever Happened to Those Prophesying Daughters?" in *A Feminist Companion to the Acts of the Apostles*, ed. Amy-Jill Levine, with Marriane Blickenstaff.

[269] On God's will, see Appendix 4 as well as Grudem, *Prophecy;* so Dunn ('Prophetic-I', 186): "Wherever in pre-Christian Judaism and early Christianity men have claimed that the words they spoke were inspired by God's Spirit, there has been an accompanying recognition that their claim might be false; wherever in pre-Christian Judaism and early Christianity prophecies have been uttered ' in the name of the Lord', the need has also been stressed for some degree of discrimination and evaluation to test and discern whether they were genuine words of the Lord or not. The question then becomes, Was a similar degree of caution exercised within the earliest Palestinian communities through and from whom the bulk of the Jesus-tradition came? Was the need to test prophetic utterances, to discriminate true from false?"

[270] He is mistaken for an Egyptian.

[271] Courtesy of poor versification at this juncture.

CHAPTER 22

1-17 THE PROGRAMMATIC STATEMENT that begins the book of Acts is undoubtedly chapter one and verse eight. It encourages witnessing. Both the noun and verb forms are related to the concept of sharing one's testimony. In chapter two we not only see how witnessing is closely associated with the proclamation of the gospel message[272] but with its defense as well. The following verses are tactfully apologetic (defending the faith):

> "Brothers and fathers, listen to the defense that I now make before you."[2] When they heard him addressing them in Hebrew, they became even more quiet 1-2) and evangelistic in character (sharing the good news:'Saul, Saul, why are you persecuting me?' [8] I answered, 'Who are you, Lord?' Then he said to me, 'I am Jesus of Nazareth[b] whom you are persecuting.' 7-8), with a strong element of personal experience and expression (testimony: I am a Jew, born in Tarsus in Cilicia, but brought up in this city at the feet of Gamaliel, educated strictly according to our ancestral law, being zealous for God,

just as all of you are today. ⁴ I persecuted this Way up to the point of death by binding both men and women and putting them in prison 3- 4). The full text follows:

Then he said: ³ "I am a Jew, born in Tarsus in Cilicia, but brought up in this city at the feet of Gamaliel, educated strictly according to our ancestral law, being zealous for God, just as all of you are today. ⁴ I persecuted this Way up to the point of death by binding both men and women and putting them in prison, ⁵ as the high priest and the whole council of elders can testify about me. From them I also received letters to the brothers in Damascus, and I went there in order to bind those who were there and to bring them back to Jerusalem for punishment.

⁶ "While I was on my way and approaching Damascus, about noon a great light from heaven suddenly shone about me. ⁷ I fell to the ground and heard a voice saying to me, 'Saul, Saul, why are you persecuting me?' ⁸ I answered, 'Who are you, Lord?' Then he said to me, 'I am Jesus of Nazareth whom you are persecuting.' ⁹ Now those who were with me saw the light but did not hear the voice of the one who was speaking to me. ¹⁰ I asked, 'What am I to do, Lord?' The Lord said to me, 'Get up and go to Damascus; there you will be told everything that has been assigned to you to do.'

¹¹ Since I could not see because of the brightness of that light, those who were with me took my hand and led me to Damascus. ¹² "A certain Ananias, who was a devout man according to the law and well-spoken of by all the Jews living there, ¹³ came to me; and standing beside me, he said, 'Brother Saul, regain your sight!' In that very hour I regained my sight and saw him. ¹⁴ Then

he said, 'The God of our ancestors has chosen you to know his will, to see the Righteous One and to hear his own voice;

¹⁵ for you will be his witness to all the world of what you have seen and heard. ¹⁶ And now why do you delay? Get up, be baptized, and have your sins washed away, calling on his name.' ¹⁷ "After I had returned to Jerusalem and while I was praying in the temple, I fell into a trance ¹⁸ and saw Jesus[c] saying to me, 'Hurry and get out of Jerusalem quickly, because they will not accept your testimony about me.' ¹⁹ And I said, 'Lord, they themselves know that in every synagogue I imprisoned and beat those who believed in you. ²⁰ And while the blood of your witness Stephen was shed, I myself was standing by, approving and keeping the coats of those who killed him.' ²¹ Then he said to me, 'Go, for I will send you far away to the Gentiles" (NRSV).

This touching testimony is rich in I-locution. Here Bock's summary is useful:

"'I was where you were' vv.3-5,

'I was called by God' (vv. 6-14),

'I was called to be a witness to the nations' (vv. 15-21).[273]

It is also worthwhile pointing out that the narrator dedicates more space to the apologetic speeches than to the apostle's sermons. Bock observes that there are "97 verses of defence speech, which represent 39 percent of the prison defence-section. This compares with 47 verses of Pauline missionary speech, or 21 percent of the missionary section." The significance of this for Bock is that "Paul the defender of the faith is as important as, if not more important than, Paul the preacher of the faith."[274]

But Paul's impressive defence speech got him nowhere, or so it seems (22-29). God's word, whether as oracle, prophecy or the like, never returns to God without achieving something. Moreover, Paul will live to fight (the good fight!) another day (30).

---

[272] "Evangelism is witnessing which confronts the uncommitted with the claims of Christ, with the hope of gaining a positive response; *Survey of Evangelism* (Kingston: Back to the Bible JA, 1988), 1.

[273] Bock, *Acts*, 659.

[274] Ibid., 655.

CHAPTER 23

1-35 IF PAUL WAS NOT so stubborn, he would have saved himself all this trouble outlined in this chapter. But then again, what do we know about God's will, especially in light of Luke 23-24: (written by the narrator, Luke) and Romans 8:28 (by Paul himself)? Some commentators say that the apostle's missionary endeavours ceased, beginning with chapter 21.[275] Paul's view, it seems to me, is that though the State or the Sanhedrin may incarcerate, the Scripture continues to liberate! (Phil 1). But defending the Faith is not always easy (1-4). If the accused lost his temper in verse 3, it appears he repented and resorted to his sense of humour in verses 5-6. Of course, Paul's 'humour', like that of his Master, is serious stuff—serious enough to have brought the house down (7). Preachers like to remind us that the failure of the Sadducees to believe[276] in the basic tenet of the resurrection was why they were *sad-u-see* (v 8). That may be so, but it does not explain the sad state of the Pharisees who were also members of the said (or sad) Sanhedrin council. Paul's happiness and joy, on the other hand, was never wrapped up primarily in his orthodoxy but in his overall posture and commitment to the will of God (Phil 4:6-13, 19).

However, it was his correct notions on the resurrection that saved his skin on this particular occasion (9), as well as the might of Rome (v 10: *The dispute became so violent that the commander was afraid Paul would be torn to pieces by them. He ordered the troops to go down and take him away from them by force and bring him into the barracks*).

In John 16:33 the people of God are warned that living this side of eternity will not always be easy, especially if doing God's will is their speciality. Paul must have been familiar with this Jesus tradition. What brought him the most comfort on this occasion is the very presence of the Lord himself (11): "*Di neks nait di Laad tan op saida Paal an tel im se, 'Tek aat, kaaz siem ou yu tel di Jeruusilem piipl dem bout mi, a siem so yu afi go tel di piipl dem iina Ruom bout mi.*" JNT

The word from the exalted Messiah had present and future force, because shortly after the divine oracle the apostle's life was in grave danger. The lives of those who plotted and fasted were at risk as well; one is only left to wonder if they lived to tell the tale. The way how Paul's life was spared (vv 12-22) reminds us of the following lyrics:

God moves in a mysterious way
His wonders to perform;

CHAPTER 23

He plants His footsteps in the sea
and rides upon the storm.
Deep in unfathomable mines
of never-failing skill
He treasures up His bright designs
And works His sovereign will.
Ye fearful saints, fresh courage take;
  The clouds ye so much dread
Are big with mercy and shall break
In blessings on your head.
Judge not the Lord by feeble sense,
  But trust Him for His grace;
  Behind a frowning providence
He hides a smiling face.
His purposes will ripen fast,
  Unfolding every hour;
  The bud may have a bitter taste,
  But sweet will be the flower.
Blind unbelief is sure to err
And scan His work in vain;
  God is His own interpreter,
And He will make it plain.[277]

God will make it plain indeed! Divine providence transfers the apostle to the Gentiles from Jerusalem in the south to Caesarea in the north; by night; with infantry; with cavalry—the best that earth could have provided, courtesy of divine sovereignty (23-35).

.

[275] E.g., Marshall, *Acts*.
[276] The Sadducees, unlike the Pharisees, also denied the existence of angels and spirits just like some theologians today. See Bock's (*Acts*) six ways of understanding v.8.
[277] http://cyberhymnal.org/htm/g/m/gmovesmw.htm.

CHAPTER 24

1-21 WITHIN A WEEK after the uproar in the south, a delegation (consisting of a high profile lawyer, the high priests, and elders) was sent to Caesarea to press charges against Paul. The prosecuting attorney appears a far better orator than Apollos of Christian fame (1-9), but in the final analysis it is the defendant (in this case Paul himself) that has real 'power of attorney'. (cf. Luke 21:12-15[278]):

> [14] But I confess this to you, that I worship the God of our ancestors according to the Way (which they call a sect), believing everything that is according to the law and that is written in the prophets. [15] I have a hope in God (a hope that these men themselves accept too) that there is going to be a resurrection of both the righteous and the unrighteous. [16] This is the reason I do my best to always have a clear conscience toward God and toward people.
>
> [17] After several years I came to bring to my people gifts for the poor and to present offerings, [18] which I was doing when they found me in the temple, ritually

purified, without a crowd or a disturbance. [19] But there are some Jews from the province of Asia who should be here before you and bring charges, if they have anything against me. [20] Or these men here should tell what crime they found me guilty of when I stood before the council, [21] other than this one thing I shouted out while I stood before them: 'I am on trial before you today concerning the resurrection of the dead'"(NET).

22-27 Having listened to the defendant carefully, the judge on this occasion adjourned the case. Felix must have heard about the personal Way (John 14:6) from Scriptures like Genesis 3:15, Deuteronomy 18 (the Law), as well as Isaiah 9:6; 53: 1-13; and Daniel 2 (the Prophets). He will hear these matters (and more!) again and again, and with a bigger audience. Paul's hope mentioned in verses 15 and 21 would surely include Daniel 12:1-3. This he was convinced of before becoming a Christian. His major concern prior to that was the Jesus of Nazareth who was hung on a tree. So he could not understand why Jesus had such a large following having been (in his mind) accursed of God.

Twenty centuries later scholarly minds like the apostle Paul still struggle with the idea, and possibility of the resurrection of Christ. Martin, for example, reminds us that the canons of modern-day historiography do not allow us to speak with any conviction regarding what the apostle himself is persuaded of. Since historical events are unrepeatable, no one can say for certain what happened back then. In some strange sort of way (that is by faith) Martin

CHAPTER 24

affirms his belief in Jesus's resurrection but not with the same type of certainty with which Paul writes (1 Cor 15) and testifies.[279]

---

[278] "[T]hey will seize you and persecute you. They will hand you over to synagogues and put you in prison, and you will be brought before kings and governors, and all on account of my name. [13] And so you will bear testimony [μαρτύριον; witness] to me. [14] But make up your mind not to worry beforehand how you will defend [ἀπολογηθῆναι·; apologetics] yourselves. [15] For I will give you words and wisdom that none of your adversaries will be able to resist or contradict." The translation 'words and wisdom' brings out the alliteration of the original (στόμα καὶ σοφίαν) nicely.

[279] Biblical Truths, 198-215.

CHAPTER 25

1-5 WHEN THE JUDICIAL machinery of any country goes awry the whole society unravels. On the surface of it the Jewish leaders appear to be seeking justice but murder is on their mind. About thirty years before they murdered the Prince of Life, and they are about to do the same thing to his chosen vessel. This chosen vessel was himself a murderer along the same lines. It is good that Festus, a representative of the state, is manifestly interested in justice and probity—at least on this occasion (5). **6-12** It's also amazing how history seems to repeat itself, for this round of trials resembles that of Stephen's, in terms of the prejudice on display (6-7).

> Then Paul made his defense: "I have done nothing wrong against the Jewish law or against the temple or against Caesar."[9] Festus, wishing to do the Jews a favour, said to Paul, "Are you willing to go up to Jerusalem and stand trial before me there on these charges?"[10] Paul answered: "I am now standing before Caesar's court, where I ought

to be tried. I have not done any wrong to the Jews, as you yourself know very well.[11] If, however, I am guilty of doing anything deserving death, I do not refuse to die. But if the charges brought against me by these Jews are not true, no one has the right to hand me over to them. I appeal to Caesar!"[12] After Festus had conferred with his council, he declared: "You have appealed to Caesar. To Caesar you will go!"

The Lord did promise that the apostle to the Gentiles would have his day in the Supreme Court, but it is doubtful that he knew how things would turn out where that is concerned. He still does not know at this juncture. He is at sea about the whole affair.[280] 13-27 Since nothing happens to the servant of God by chance, we are not surprised that the next trial date affords Paul the opportunity to speak to more people with political clout (13-22). Dr Luke captures the moment with these words: "On the following day Agrippa and Bernice made their entrance into the assembly hall, along with the military officers of high rank and some other prominent people, with much pomp and pride[281] (φαντασίας,[282] *phantasias*)" (v 23). And having summoned the detainee, Festus opened a new round of cross examination with these opening remarks:

> King Agrippa, and all you gentlemen here present with us, you see this man about whom all the people of the Jews appealed to me, both at Jerusalem and here, loudly declaring that he ought not to live any longer. [25] But I found that he had committed nothing worthy of death;

CHAPTER 25

and since he himself appealed to [p]the Emperor, I decided to send him. 26

Yet I have nothing definite about him to write to my lord. Therefore, I have brought him before you all and especially before you, King Agrippa, so that after the investigation has taken place, I may have something to write. 27 For it seems absurd to me in sending a prisoner, not to indicate also the charges against him (NASB).

---

[280] For the next three chapters!
[281] The hendiadys is from a Jamaican Festival song by Toots and the Maytals.
[282] "Pomp," *The UBS Greek NT* (Stuttgart: Deutsche Bibelgesellschaft), 400. The word "Pomp" is from the Greek *pompē*; in Old English it means 'vain and boastful display,' according to the *Concise Oxford English Dictionary*.

CHAPTER 26

1-18 AFTER RECEIVING PERMISSION to speak (in Greek? v.1), Paul proceeds to share his revolutionary experience; and for the first time we are explicitly told that the resurrected Lord spoke in a Semitic tongue (v.14; 'Hebrew language' [RSV]; 'Aramaic' [NIV]). Again we have the contrastive *egō* . . . *egō* (I ... I), as in 22:8. The fact that *egō*, is placed on the lips of Jesus in all three Lukan passages seems to justify Dalman's Aramaic reconstruction of *'anā Yēshûa'* (I am Yeshua),[283] as well as shows Luke's interest in the Dominical[284] 'I'.

What appears certain here is that Jesus spoke a Semitic language,[285] at least on this occasion, and the dominical 'I' has definitely played a prominent role in the dialogue. One could say that *egō* not only adorned the authority of the Dominical 'I' but also points in the direction of his divinity as well (*I am Jesus whom you persecute*; v. 15, is preceded by *'Lord'*).[286] This no doubt left an indelible impression on Saul, and his own employment of 'I' would never approach anything like what he encountered on the Damascus road. From now on there is only one Supreme 'I' (*egō* [ἐγώ]; 17) clothed in humanity—the one who spoke from heaven about his love for the Gentiles.[287] An interesting observation is the apostle's own use of *egō* in verse 10 (cf. 22:3), and especially in verses 9 and 15 where it is set in contrast to a dominical 'I'.

This Pauline 'I' is undoubtedly auto-biographical. Verses 4-11 correspond well with another testimony written in a different genre and for a different purpose:

> If someone else thinks they have reasons to put confidence in the flesh, I have more: [5] circumcised on the eighth day, of the people of Israel, of the tribe of Benjamin, a Hebrew of Hebrews; in regard to the law, a Pharisee; [6] as for zeal, persecuting the church; as for righteousness based on the law, faultless (Phil. 3:4b-6 NIV).

But everything changed about 12:12pm that day while Saul and his 'swords-men' saw a light

> from heaven, brighter than the sun, blazing around me and my companions. [14] We all fell to the ground, and I heard a voice saying to me in Aramaic,[a] 'Saul, Saul, why do you persecute me? It is hard for you to kick against the goads' (12-14 NIV).

The commission that was given on that occasion reveals important insights into Luke's soteriology: for the writer, salvation is an eye-opening experience (cf. 2 Cor 4:4-6) which involves a turning from spiritual darkness to the light of God's kingdom (John 8); it inevitably results in freedom (*from the power of Satan to God*) and forgiveness, as well as positional and practical holiness (16-18). The narrator continues:

> [19] "So then, King Agrippa, I was not disobedient to the vision from heaven. [20] First to those in Damascus, then to those in Jerusalem and in all Judea, and then to the Gentiles, I preached that they should repent and turn to God and demonstrate their repentance by their deeds. [21] That is why some Jews seized me in the temple courts and tried to kill me. [22] But God has helped me to this very day; so I stand here and testify to small and great alike. I am saying nothing beyond what the prophets and Moses said would happen— [23] that the Messiah would suffer and, as the first to rise from the dead, would bring the message of light to his own people and to the Gentiles." [24] At this point Festus interrupted Paul's defense. "You are out of your mind, Paul!" he shouted. "Your great learning is driving you insane."
>
> [25] "I am not insane, most excellent Festus," Paul replied. "What I am saying is true and reasonable. [26] The king is familiar with these things, and I can speak freely to him. I am convinced that none of this has escaped his notice, because it was not done in a corner. [27] King Agrippa, do you believe the prophets? I know you do."[28] Then Agrippa said to Paul, "Do you think that in such a short time you can persuade me to be a Christian?"

²⁹ Paul replied, "Short time or long—I pray to God that not only you but all who are listening to me today may become what I am, except for these chains."³⁰ The king rose, and with him the governor and Bernice and those sitting with them. ³¹ After they left the room, they began saying to one another, "This man is not doing anything that deserves death or imprisonment."³² Agrippa said to Festus, "This man could have been set free if he had not appealed to Caesar." (NIV).

---

²⁸³ (2004, 241)

²⁸⁴ Lordship.

²⁸⁵ On this question, see Ken M. Penner "Ancient Names for Hebrew and Aramaic: A Case for Lexical Revision," *NTS* 65.3 (July 2019): 412-423. His summary on page 412 reads as follows:

> The view expressed in BDAG that *Hebrais* refers not to Hebrew but to 'the Aramaic spoken at that time in Palestine' derives from a century-old argument that because *Hebrais* could mean either Aramaic or Hebrew, and since the average person could not understand Hebrew, *Hebrais* must mean Aramaic. This article challenges the view that *Hebrais(ti)* could mean Aramaic (1) by using an exhaustive list of all instances to show that Aramaic was consistently distinguished from Hebrew, and (2) by explaining the evidence to the contrary: Aramaic-looking words in John, Josephus and Philo that are said to be *Hebraisti*.

²⁸⁶ Dalman The Words of Jesus, 330. Mit . . . hebräischen Sprache . . . in welcher nach Apg. 21, 40; 22, 2 Paulus zu den Jerusalemern, nach 26, 14 Jesus zu Paulus redete, wird das Aramäische gemeint sein (Dalman 1965, 5)/'Aramaic . . . must be meant by the "Hebrew tongue" in which . . . Jesus spoke to Paul (Acts 26: [14])' (Dalman 1997, 7). As above, another of Dalman's (1967, 17) original reads: 'anā jēshûa'/Ich bin Jesus.

CHAPTER 26

We therefore cannot agree with the following Johannine assessment by Dunn: "Had the striking 'I am' self-assertions . . . been remembered as spoken by Jesus, how could any Evangelist have ignored them so completely as the Synoptics do?'. But see Luke's (7: 27) intriguing omission of *egō* , from Malachi 3:1 (LXX). But see Luke's (7: 27) intriguing omission of *egō*, from Malachi 3:1 (LXX).

' The NRSV has the identical rendering accompanied with a marginal note that reads "That is, Aramaic". The NLT has just the opposite, and the REB with its 'Jewish language' is non-committal.

[287] "We have seen that Paul's previous self-concept portrayed the features of someone who was highly satisfied with his religious achievements. This self-appraisal was totally shattered by the Damascus event. ...He realized that, because of human sin, man not only has no ground for any selfboasting before God (Rom 3: 27; 4:2; [7: 1-25] 2 Cor 12:5); he is totally and irrevocably dependent on *grace* [as a spiritual weakling. Therefore] Paul's new self- understanding [as dependent 'I'] also becomes clear in the radical way in which he understands himself as transformed by God" (du Toit 1996, 84; my italics).

CHAPTER 27

1-12 FINALLY, PAUL IS ON his way to Rome, not on a cruise liner, but on a rugged first century vessel, along with Luke his friend and private physician, a Thessalonian brother, and fellow prisoners. Dr Luke is careful to note how Paul is singled out for special treatment—an early line of evidence that the Lord himself is with them (1-3). Luke will continue to provide details of the voyage to Rome with his mention of places like Asia Minor (a part of Turkey today), Thessalonica (a part of Greece), Sidon (a part of Lebanon), Cyprus, Cilicia and Pamphylia, Myra, Lycia, Cnidus, Crete, Salmone, Phoenix, and "a place called Fair Havens, near the town of Lasea." He also makes mention of relatively minor challenges along the way (6-9).

In Luke chapter 5 we have a carpenter (or builder) telling a seasoned fisherman where to cast his nets; now in verse 10 we have a tent-maker (leather worker) instructing seasoned sailors about the high seas. In Luke 5 the fisherman listened to the carpenter and was flabbergasted—penitent even! Here the Roman officer ignores the advice of the prisoner. This is understandable.

Little does he know that the said prisoner is reflecting the mind of God (9-12; cf. John 1:11, 14, 18). On account of the fact that only a gentle breeze was blowing from the south, the chief stakeholders on board thought that they are relatively safe. So they pull up the anchor and continue their journey. However, they did not throw caution to the wind, gentle or not. They made every effort to keep as close as possible to the Cretan shore (13). But not too long after that, another

> wind of hurricane force,[288] called the Northeaster, swept down from the island. [15] The ship was caught by the storm and could not head into the wind; so we gave way to it and were driven along. [16] As we passed to the lee of a small island called Cauda, we were hardly able to make the lifeboat secure, [17] so the men hoisted it aboard. Then they passed ropes under the ship itself to hold it together. Because they were afraid they would run aground on the sandbars of Syrtis, they lowered the sea anchor[b] and let the ship be driven along. [18] We took such a violent battering from the storm that the next day they began to throw the cargo overboard. [19] On the third day, they threw the ship's tackle overboard with their own hands. [20] When neither sun nor stars appeared for many days and the storm continued raging, we finally gave up all hope of being saved.[289]

CHAPTER 27

The verses above (particularly v. 20) paint a very bleak picture—one of hopelessness. So Paul's (on the surface of it) I-told-you-so posture and pronouncement come across as a bit callous (21). But when we read verse 21 in light of what follows, we see the glimmer at the end of the tunnel, or better, the sunrise on the horizon (after that dark night of the soul. 22-25). Gaventa[290] divides the voyage into seven 'sea' sections, which we have rebranded:

- Difficulties (vv 1-8)
- Disappointment (9-12)
- Disaster (13-20)
- Declaration (21-26)
- Despair (27-32)
- Decisiveness (33-38)
- Destruction (39-44)

---

[288] This forms an inclusio with the sound of a hurricane in chapter 2 (second chapter with the second to last).
[289] "wi did shuor se wi don fa, notn kudn siev wi" JNT.
[290] *Acts*, 350.

CHAPTER 28

1-31 THIS ENDING CHAPTER begins with some good news—the fulfilment of prophecy that no life would be lost. The ship was destroyed but all are 'now on board' on the island of Malta, with showers of blessing from above and from below. They are safe but cold. So warm-hearted Paul (prisoner though he may be) decides to share the warmth, but a viper took a liking to him to the point where the philanthropic islanders misinterpreted the situation. Yes, Paul was once a murderer; but now he's a changed hombre. Through Christ and the Spirit he shares his life (1-10; cf. Phil. 4:13).

Certainly, from a literary point of view this is the end of the journey for Paul. That's where the writer locates him. That is where the apostle was headed. There are more opportunities in Rome for apologetics and witnessing, courtesy of divine providence (11-29).[291]

Then Paul dwelt two whole years in his own rented house, and received all who came to him, 31 preaching the kingdom of God and teaching the things which concern the Lord Jesus Christ with all confidence, no one forbidding him.

Summary and Conclusion

One of the ways in which the Lukan plot is advanced in Acts is by the provision of a variety of progress reports. These reports serve the trajectory of his narrative which moves inexorably from the religious capital (Jerusalem) to the imperial capital that was no less religious but much more pluralistic in orientation. A central part of the narrative juxtaposes the conversions of three prominent individuals who appear to be descendants of Ham, Shem and Japheth, the three men given the primary responsibility of re-populating the earth, according to the Genesis record.[292]

After citing a few instances of 'mass' conversions, Luke begins his triadic show-piece by telling the story of a Gentile treasurer, who may well have been regarded as among the first-fruits of the promise found in Psalm 68:31 (Acts 8). The third example of an individual coming under the influence of the Messiah (chapter 10) appears to be an adumbration of the final episode of Acts which is located in Rome. The centre-piece within the triad indicates Luke's main interest in the former Semitic zealot who became the chief agent in carrying the evangel beyond the borders of Palestine into the very centre of the evil Empire.

CHAPTER 28

Saul of Tarsus, then, becomes for Luke the best example of a person who has fully committed herself or himself to the redemptive and imposing Messianic Presence whose power is mediated through the Pentecostal Spirit. This fact can be easily borne out by the amount of space (an estimated two-thirds of Luke's material) dedicated to the apostle. From chapter 13 to the end, then, Paul has been Luke's hero.[293] Now the hero is in Rome. Why Rome? Kilgallen's response to this query is worth considering:

One of the teachings to Theophilus in this tumultuous century is, it seems most likely, an explanation as to how it is that he, a pagan, has become a full member of an exclusionary religion that began as thoroughly Jewish. This attention to Theophilus, it is suggested, makes necessary a story that geographically and chronologically arrives and finishes at the place where Theophilus and his community are; it is to them the story is written (Luke 1, 4). Luke's work does not stop till Rome, 61 AD, but stops there and then. This strongly suggests Luke's satisfaction that he has told a story which finally arrives where Theophilus is. That Luke stops his work at Rome, 61 AD indicates Theophilus and his church are there. By Luke's story, Theophilus understands the truth many teachings, particularly about his place in God's plan of salvation.[294]

There is a sense in which the book of Acts is a tale of two cities: Jerusalem and Rome. The former was one of the largest centres of Jewry; the latter was an urban area of around a million people, roughly half of whom were slaves.[295] Both in Luke's first and last chiastic frames (A-

A')[296] he has the willing-and winning God reaching down and reaching out to "the poor . . . the prisoners . . . the blind . . . [and] the oppressed," and others (Luke 4:18) in the most significant metropolitan areas.[297] It is a sacrificial venture. If the Messiah (Act 2:23) and Stephen (Acts 7:54-59) die in Jerusalem, Peter and Paul will die in Rome. The deaths of these witnesses did not signal the end of the Way (John 14:6 admits no cul-de-sac). They point to a new beginning. Put another way, Rome makes way for new frontiers (cf. Rom 1: 1-16).[298] So the apostle's willingness to go to Rome was an assault[299] on the capital of Empire, not to take life but to give life through the One whose life was taken by Rome.

In chapter 28:30, Paul's willingness was matched by that of his visitors, and, in a sense, by Rome in allowing him the privilege of proclaiming another king and kingdom (28:31).If Luke's first volume begins with the anointed One *par excellence* (Luke 4:18), his second ends with another anointed (Acts 13:46; Isa 49:6) who takes his paradigmatic role with the utmost seriousness (e.g., 1 Cor 11:1). So does Luke. And it was after the first missionary journey of Barnabas and Paul, sent out from Antioch, that Luke reports the first major theological and missiological discussion, involving the two main centres of Christianity at the time. After the apostolic council and the promulgation of the first and foremost of letters of earliest Christianity, Luke began to narrow his focus on the life of one missionary whose training and commissioning made him especially equipped to embody and expound the significance of the Jerusalem-council letter that has so much import for the Messianic community in general and Gentile Christianity in particular.

So, in this commentary, I have posited that Luke employed chiasmus[300] to delineate the way in which the gospel reached Rome from Jerusalem.[301] The structure highlights certain divine initiatives[302] (two centrifugal and two centripetal) that engaged the Messianic community in a dominically motivated mission. A fifth initiative, the centrepiece of the macrostructure, focuses attention on the importance of theological discussion for the enterprise of gospel contextualization. Finally, Luke's two volumes end the way they began, with both the prologue (Luke 1:1-4) and the epilogue (Acts 28:30-31) marked by a certain weightiness of literary style that forms an unmistakable inclusion.[303]

---

[291] Seen here as the outworking of God's plan (26:30-32; cf. 2:23), about which Luke has much to say (e.g., 27:21-25; see also D.G. Peterson, *The Acts of the Apostles* [PNTC; Grand Rapids: Eerdmans, 2009], 29-32).

[292] On these see J. Daniel Hayes, *From Every People and Nation: A Biblical Theology of Race* (Leicester: Apollos, 2003), 51-65, 157-180.

[293] For an interesting take on this hero, see Brittany E. Wilson, "The Blinding of Paul and the Power of God: Masculinity, Sight, and Self-Control in Acts 9," *JBL* 133 (2014): 367-387.

[294] John Kilgallen, "Luke Wrote to Rome—a Suggestion," *Biblica* 88 (2007), 255. For a credible proposal as to why Luke is silent on the outcome of Paul's trial in Rome, see Daniel Marguerat, "The End of Acts (28:16-31) and the Rhetoric of Silence," in S.E. Porter and T.H. Olbricht, eds., *Rhetoric and the NT: Essays from the 1992 Heidelbeg Conference* (Sheffield: SAP, 1993), 74-89. In one of her latest papers ("Imaging the Divine: Idolatry and God's Body in the Book of Acts," *NTS* [May 2019]), she writes (unconvincingly in my estimation):

This article problematises the widespread assumption that the God of early Christianity is an invisible God. This assumption is found in both popular and academic discourse and often appeals to biblical critiques of divine images to make its case. Yet while Hebrew Bible scholars have recently questioned this axiomatic belief, New Testament scholars have yet to do the same. To address this oversight, this article first looks at divine images and idol polemic in the ancient world and then turns to Luke's depiction of divine images in the book of Acts as a test case. Here I demonstrate how Acts depicts God as a visible – and even embodied – being, while at the same time critiquing visual representations of the divine. With Acts, we find that not all Christians 'imaged' God as invisible

---

[295] Stanley Porter, The Letter to the Romans: A linguistic and Literary Commentary (Sheffield: Phoenix, 2015), 4.

[296] The other points of the frame, especially B-B´, are suffused in the book of Acts.

[297] On God's heart for the upper echelon of Roman society, see James Edwards, "'Public Theology' in Luke-Acts: The Witness of the Gospel to Powers and Authorities," NTS 62 / Issue 02 (April 2016): 227 – 252.

[298] If Christianity back then was "turning the world upside down" and if in the twentieth century it was the opiate of the people, it remains today an equal opportunity 'fix'; what it did to Rome it will do to other cities. For example, Luke's trajectory takes us from the monotheistic capital in the east (Jerusalem) to the polytheistic centre of the west (Rome), with a brief stop at the 'unknown god' city of Athens. Luke wrote after the dispatch of the book of Romans, knowing fully well that the Gospel left none of these cities untouched (A Christocentric and triune monotheism captured the imagination of many). If he were/was familiar with Ephesians, he would have known that Artemis of Ephesus was unfavourably compared with the people of God in 2:10. In other words, if the temple of Diana was one of the seven won-

CHAPTER 28

ders of the world, God's 'poem' outlasted it, and is the only temple that will make it into eternity (Matt 16:18).

[299]Like Mark's gospel and Priscilla's homily that has come down to us as the book of Hebrews, and drafted by her male amanuensis (Heb. 13).

[300]In commenting on Luke 9:6, Darrell Bock(*Luke 1:1-9:50*, vol. 1 [Grand Rapids: Baker, 1994], 817-818) comments: "By way of conclusion, Luke summarizes the mission briefly by referring to two primary tasks of the twelve: preaching the good news and healing (so also Acts 13:3 with 14:1-18). These are the same two categories with which Luke introduced the passage (Luke 9:1-2), except that he now gives them in reverse order (9:2 also spoke about the kingdom). The summary thus forms an *inclusio* with the introduction (Bovon 1989: 460). Some have pointed out the *inclusio* of Acts 1:6 ("kingdom") and 28:31 ("kingdom"); and the "reverse order" relative to the relevant Lukan mission mentioned by Bock appears to parallel the purported macro-structure of Luke's second volume.

[301]See https://biblicalstudies.org.uk/pdf/cjet/17_094.pdf. For the chiasmus; and for one that includes the Lukan Gospel, see Kenneth R. Wolfe, "The Chiastic Structure of Luke-Acts and Some Implications for Worship," *Southwestern Journal of Theology* 30 (Spring, 1980): 62-63.

[302]See also Beverly Gaventa, "Initiatives Divine and Human in the Story World of Acts," in G.N. Stanton et al. eds., *The Holy Spirit and Christian Origins* (Grand Rapids: Eerdmans, 2004), 79-89. According to J.B. Green (*The Gospel of Luke* [Grand Rapids: Eerdmans, 1997], 830), "[T]he story of Luke-Acts is, in large part, the tale of two competing purposes---that of God and that which opposes God."

[303] J. Nolland, *Luke 1-9:*20 (Waco, Texas, 1989), 4.

APPENDIX 1

The Apostle Paul and the Church

ALTHOUGH PAUL, in and around 49 A.D, founded the set of churches in South Galatia,[304] he is definitely not the founder of Christianity, as Richard Dawkins claims.[305] Matthew 16 and Acts chapters 1-2 are far better witnesses where the origin of the Messianic community is concerned. Though not as great as the founder of the Christian faith, in the minds of many, the Apostle Paul is the greatest missionary the world has ever seen. Even if we disagree with this judgement there can be no doubt regarding the tremendous impact he has made in advancing the cause of Christ in our world.

Yet, in the words of Dr Tucker, "Paul is a less awesome figure than some adulatory devotees would have him to be. In many ways, he was a very ordinary man facing ordinary problems that have confronted missionaries ever since."[306] This observation, paradoxically, serves to highlight the Apostle's greatness even more, for if he was so ordinary, whence his greatness as a missionary? An examination of the Apostle Paul's role as an evangelist, Pastor and teacher may furnish the answer to the above query.

Paul was an evangelist indeed. But he was not always so, because he once sought to impede the progress of the Gospel of Jesus Christ. He relentlessly persecuted the people of God until he himself submitted to the Lord of Glory one bright and sunny day on the way to the city of Damascus. It was the Lord who announced to Ananias that this once proud Pharisee would be an evangelist. "GO! This man is my chosen instrument to carry my Name before the Gentiles and their kings before the people of Israel," was the heavenly injunction.

It was not very long before the now converted Saul began preaching the good news of Christ in Damascus, showing convincingly that Jesus who was crucified was indeed the awaited Messiah (Acts 9:19-22). He began, quite naturally, with his own people. However, his effort was greeted with almost immediate opposition.

Sometime after this bitter experience the Apostle Paul began to have a more or less settled ministry in the thriving assembly at Antioch. It was from this church that he received further direction through the Spirit to be involved in a wider ministry. He was to embark on a missionary career that would take him as far as Rome, the capital of the world, and he was to henceforth serve not as a loner, but as a labourer among many. His evangelistic partner from the home base was Barnabas—the man who was instrumental in gaining an entry for him among the believers at Jerusalem.

APPENDIX 1

Having left the church at Antioch to fulfil their missionary vocation, Barnabas and Saul stopped in Salamis, after passing through Seleucia on the mainland. Salamis was a city on the isle of Cyprus which boasted an apparently large community of Jews, so "they preached the Word of God in the synagogues" (Acts 13:6).

If evangelism is witnessing that confronts the uncommitted with the claims of Jesus Christ, then Paul was an evangelist *par excellence*. As a fisher of men he went where the fish were and as a result he was constantly found in the synagogues where there was always a gathering of Jews with their proselytes, "For Moses of old times hath in every city them that preach him, being read in the synagogues every Sabbath day" (Acts 15:21).

But Paul in particular was not just acting out a principle. He was expressing a heartfelt concern for first century Jewry. He confessed: "I say the truth in Christ, I lie not, my conscience also bearing me witness in the Holy Ghost, that I have great heaviness and continual sorrow in my heart. For I could, that I myself were accursed from Christ for my brethren, my kinsmen according to the flesh: who are Israelites" (Rom. 9:1-4a).

However, while the apostle Paul had the privilege of seeing a number of Jews coming to the Lord, his greater success was with the Gentiles. And as he moved along, he evangelized, preached, argued, testified, and persuaded his non-Jewish audiences (e.g. Acts 17: 1ff; 26:27ff). The missionary activities of the Apostle Paul were not confined to evangelism alone but included a calculated effort to foster the spiritual development of new believers.

Even before Paul went on his first missionary journey the importance of nourishing babes of the faith was impressed on him when he first visited the church of Antioch. A revival had broken out in that city after certain itinerant evangelists powerfully proclaimed the gospel to both the Jewish and Gentile inhabitants. News of this activity reached Jerusalem, and the church there sent Barnabas to conduct follow-up work.

After being involved in some intensive counselling sessions with the new believers and seeing further numerical growth, Barnabas decided to instruct them more accurately in the things of the Lord. To help him accomplish this task, he enlisted the help of Saul of Tarsus, a man in whom he had discerned the gift of teaching. "And when he had found him, he brought him unto Antioch. And it came to pass that for a whole year they assembled themselves with the church, and taught much people. And the disciples were called Christians first in Antioch" (Acts 11:26).

This must have been a memorable experience for Paul, because as a result of this concentrated teaching the disciples were dubbed "Christians". Their fellowmen had seen a difference in their life-style. There was no doubt in the young teacher's mind that there was a close connection between the nickname CHRISTIAN and the creed he and Barnabas had so faithfully expounded. Later on in his writing to the church at Ephesus he had clearly thought-out philosophy of edification.

APPENDIX 1

The flow of Paul's thought expressed in chapter 4:11-15 is as follows: The risen and glorified Christ has given certain gifted persons to His church (v. 11); The task of these persons is to equip the saints for service (v.12a); The involvement of the saints in the ministry is with a view "to the edifying of the body of Christ ... till we all come ... unto the measure of the statue of the fullness of Christ" (vv. 12b, 13).

Paul's plan to see the maturity of God's people was squarely based on the Word of God. Writing to Timothy just before his martyrdom he reminds the young pastor of the authenticity and potency of Scripture (2 Tim. 3:15-17) and proceeded thereafter to urge its proclamation. With a note of sadness, the aged Apostle anticipated a time when even saints will resist any effort made to ensure genuine spiritual maturity (2 Tim. 4:1-4).

Prior to writing this epistle to his young companion, he had met briefly with the Ephesian Elders en route to Rome. In this solemn meeting the ten-making missionary who was instrumental in founding the church at Ephesus, unburdened his heart to the elders of that church. His heart was for their survival. Committed as he was to spiritual development, his concern went beyond this: he wanted to leave behind a vibrant, God-glorifying church that would make him proud at the BEMA (cf. 1 Thess. 2:19).

It is in this light that we must understand Paul's discourse at Miletus.

> And from Miletus he sent to Ephesus, and called the elders of the church. And when they were come to him, he said unto them, Ye know, from the first day that I came into Asia, after what manner I have been with you at all seasons, serving the Lord with all humility of mind, and with many tears, and temptations, which befell me by the lying in wait of the Jews: and how I kept back nothing that was profitable to you, but have shewed you, and have taught you publicly, and from house to house...Wherefore I take you to record this day, that I am pure from the blood of all men. For I have not shunned to declare unto all the counsel of God (Acts 20:17-20, 26-27).

Yet another aspect of Paul's concern for the people of God is seen in his prayer life. If, as the epigram goes, "intercession is love on its knees," then there is no doubt that the Apostle to the Gentiles really loved his converts. It is worthy of note that in most of his epistles written from prison, prayers are mentioned at the beginning and end of the letters. (Eph. 1:3f, 6:18f; Phl. 1:3f, 4:6; Col. 1:9f, 4:1).

Paul's prayer for the Colossians is quite significant in the light of the fact that he did not start that assembly. He was so committed to helping people attain Christ-likeness that he constantly cried out to God, who alone can effect any lasting change in human nature.

Did the Apostle Paul have any plan to ensure that the church through-out her history would have a true "Apostolic" succession – that is, an unbroken line of leaders who

APPENDIX 1

would genuinely care for God's heritage? And if so, what is it? I believe that the answer to the first question is in the affirmative. The balance of this article attempts to address the second.

Already in Paul's day there was a shortage of Christian leaders. He could say to Timothy, his trusted co-labourer, "Do thy diligence to come shortly unto me: for Demas hath forsaken me, having loved this world, and is departed unto Thessalonica" (2 Tim. 4:9-10).

It must have been with tears in his eyes he penned these words to the Philippians Christians, "But I trust in the Lord Jesus to send Timothy shortly unto you, that I also maybe of good comfort, when I know your state. For I have no man likeminded, who will naturally care for your state. For all seek their own, not the things which are Jesus Christ's."

But if this was indeed the case in the first century church it was not Paul's fault, for it is evident from a study of his ministry that one of his priorities was the training of Christian leaders. This he sought to do by way of positive example. Once again, we turn to Acts 20:17-35. What Paul did among the early converts at Ephesus was not accidental.

Evidently from 2 Timothy 2:2, Paul had a class of specially handpicked people whom he trained to carry the burden of the ministry in the succeeding generation. Every believer should be concerned about telling the gospel to others. However, this passage is particularly applicable to leaders.

Every such servant of God, while not neglecting the whole congregation, should endeavour to develop other leaders who will be qualified and competent to carry the gospel effectively to others. This is how the gospel reached us. It is our responsibility to prepare others to reach the next generation.

What was Paul's curriculum for potential Church leaders like? This we are not explicitly told, but from his various emphases here and there in the New Testament it may be possible to put together a fairly accurate picture of at least his "core disciplines."

We can be fairly certain that such a curriculum, if it ever existed, was squarely based on the sacred writings. It is highly improbable that the young pastor at Ephesus was hearing the words of 2 Timothy 2:2 for the first time. The apostle must have imparted to his students sound Bible study principles, drawing both from his rabbinic and Christian traditions.

In some places we find this missionary theologian stressing (rather than straining) certain points of grammar (eg. The singular number in Gal 3:16). He wanted Timothy to give heed to "sound words" (11 Tim. 1:13).

Imprisonment itself and impending execution did not stop the apostle Paul from serious study of God's Word (11 Tim. 4). This must have had a tremendous effect on his student, Timothy.

As a missionary, the Apostle Paul was faithful both to his evangelistic call and his follow-up efforts. He also sought to reproduce himself in men and women ("men"

APPENDIX 1

generic in 2 Tim. 2:2) who would carry the torch of leadership to yet another generation of believers.

It is the apostle's work in these three areas that made him great in our judgement. It seems evident then that Paul was consciously carrying out in his ministry what is commonly known as the great commission (Matt. 28:18-20, et cetera; cf. Jn. 14:15; 2 Cor. 5:14). What the apostle Paul and others did for the first century is left for us to do in the twenty-first.

---

[304]Schweiser, Eduard, *A Theological Introduction to the New Testament*. Translated by O. R. Dean, Jr. (London: SPCK 1992), 73.

[305]The God Delusion, 58.

[306] Ruth Tucker, *From Jerusalem to Irian Jaya* (Grand Rapids: Zondervan, 2004), 27.

APPENDIX 2
CAFU

Chronological Survey

FORTY YEARS BEFORE Pogba and company won the World Cup, the Christian Ambassadors Footballers United (CAFU) came into being with the express purpose of reaching other men with the Gospel. The movement first started with a group of Christians from Maranatha Gospel Hall in the Vineyard Town-Franklyn Town community, who was desirous of entering a team in the local corner league competition. Later Christians from other churches were invited to participate to strengthen the team and before long a ministry of rich inter-denominational endeavour was born.

Over the years CAFU has engaged Manning Cup, Major League, Premier League and other teams in order to spread the word. CAFU has also entered a few competitions, namely, the former Red Label league, as well as the Tourers and Masters League competitions, all under the auspices of the JFF. Twice in the 80s the squad travelled to Washington D.C. to enter the annual Bob Marley tournament. In October 98 CAFU toured Cuba, and in 2003 and 2006, Orlando.

Today the group is now divided into two squads, one bearing the name M V (Men of Vision) Exodus and the other bearing the original Christian Ambassadors label. This has resulted in a more effective witness. Both squads are made up of pastors, lecturers, physicians, engineers, students, attorneys, artisans, accountants, business men, technical directors (formerly Rene Simoes and Carl Brown), a translator, one scientist and a few unemployed. A chapter of CAFU was established in Florida in the 90s and there are plans afoot to do the same for Boston, Toronto and New York. Another tour is also planned for Orlando in short order. Like the local church, CAFU seeks to be always self-governing, self-supporting, and of course, self-propagating in its auxiliary ministry.

Canonical Support

Superficially, CAFU is encouraged by a text like John 4 which talks about the 'fields' (football, that is) that are white and ready to harvest. Members of both squads are also impressed with the 'beautiful feet' which are mentioned in connection with the evangel expounded in Romans (10:15).

Substantially, it is recognized that reaching men is a much more daunting task than is first realized. Ever since

APPENDIX 2

the 'seed' (masculine in the original) was announced in Genesis 3:15 there has been a conspiracy of the enemy to madden some males (like Cain) and murder others (like Abel; ever wondered why Cain killed Abel, without cable? Check out 1 John 3:11). Either way there was an attempt to prevent the 'Bruiser' from carrying out his work. Witness as a well the work of Pharaoh in Exodus 1 and the move of Herod in Matthew 2.

Of course, Satan did not prevent the Seed from accomplishing his task (Colossians 2:15), but this does not prevent the enemy from unleashing his fury against all who have the same gender of his Bruiser. After all, the more youths he kills the fewer will benefit from the salvific achievement of Calvary. I very well believe that this dynamic goes a far way in explaining the spiralling murder rate in our country—and elsewhere (a case of *caan ketch Quaku yu ketch im shut?*). It may also partially explain why males are marginalizing other males and why the educational system does not seem to be working for 'mankind' in Jamaica. Most certainly the prevalence of illegal drugs particularly among the male population is more than a pharmaceutical matter. It is spiritual to the core.

If the forgoing thesis is correct it is understandable why Christ laid such emphasis on the calling and training of men, why he concentrated his efforts in the area of Galilee, which could be considered the 'ghetto/inner-city' of Palestine in those days. A similar emphasis for women was hardly needed, since they routinely came for help (Luke 7:36ff) and readily understood his mission (John 12:1ff). The contrast of the male disciples would have been hilarious if it was not so serious (John 18:1ff). It is no wonder that James likens the disobedient to a male who looks in the mirror and promptly forgets to make the requisite adjustments (James 1:23ff). Neither 1st females nor 21st women are in the habit of doing that.

The thesis also adds meaning to the enigmatic phrase, 'the disciple whom Jesus loved.' Why was this disciple given this special privilege? Was he that special? Was it because his family was wealthy? When I first made my probe of these questions, I knew from the outset that there was no partiality on the part of the Master. So why then was John known as the disciple whom Jesus loved? The answer to this question I found revealing.

When John and his brother James first met the Lord they were nicknamed sons of thunder. The new name was hardly complimentary. It was more descriptive of their fiery and misplaced zeal more than anything else. In a fairly objective profile of these sons of Zebedee, the gentile Gospel writer, Luke, enlightens our darkness in chapter 9 of his first volume. In verse 46 we are told of a heated discussion among the disciples concerning bragging rights. (It is Matthew's gospel that informs us as to what precipitated the quarrel. The boys' mother had come requesting special (cabinet?) privileges for her sons. And the other disciples were indignant.

Possibly, James and John must have openly supported and defended mom's request. What exactly Jesus perceived in their hearts we are not told. But whatever it was warranted a mild rebuke (Luke 9:46-48). What I find intriguing is that it was John who stood to give the 'vote of thanks' in the following verse. Well not quite. Verse 49 appears to present John as making some attempt to redeem himself. After all, if *yu trow stone inna pigpen di fus wan whey bawl out a im get lick*! But John should have kept his mouth shut. Here comes another rebuke in verse 50.

Jesus and his disciples are now on their way to the capital city. Needing visas to pass through central Palestine, messengers were sent to the Samaritan embassy (v. 52). The application was promptly turned down. No surprise here, for Jews have no dealing with Samaritans (today it is the Palestinians!). 'And when his disciples James and John saw it, they said, "Lord, do you want us to command fire to come down from heaven and consume them?"' (v. 54). Sons of thunder indeed! Needless to say, another rebuke follows (vv. 55-56).

Personally speaking, if I were Jesus John could never be a part of my apostolic band in training much more to be known as the disciple whom I love dearly! Neither James nor Peter who completed the unholy trinity. All three were from Galilee known in those days for its pugnacious and foul-mouthed citizens. If Peter's denial of his Master was accompanied with expletives, we are not surprised. He was Galilean. If Peter was aiming for the head of Malchus, we are not surprised. He was brought up in Galilee, and can anything good come out of any of its towns (John 1:46)?

So why then was John so privileged? To reach men in general special effort must be made. But to reach really bad men like Peter, James and John special effort must be doubled. Whenever the Lord went on a special mission, he would take three of his students with him (guess which three?) for at least two reasons: 1) it was too much risk to leave them behind, and 2) because his brand of love is tailor-made for sinners (Rom. 5:8).

APPENDIX 3

Reflections on Theological Education

Rev'd Anthony Chung (Pastor of the Ridgemount United Church, Mandeville, JA)

EVERY EDUCATIONAL ENDEAVOR has some distinctive and undergirding philosophy upon which it is based. It is this distinctive that sets it apart from the others. Such is the case with theological education. We in theological education feel that there is something in our field that sets us apart from the rest. What are the distinctives? Or, to put it another way: What is it that makes "theological education," theological education? After pursuing theological education for over four years, I have given thought to this question as it relates to what theological education *must* do.

Firstly, theological education must make the student intellectually proficient. By this I mean that our minds and thinking capacities must be expanded and widened as we pursue theological education. As theological students we must be able to examine the issues critically and see what is really at stake; what is central and what is peripheral.

Intellectual proficiency means being able to present well thought-out and well-reasoned positions on the pertinent issues. The Bible is clear that we are called to use our minds. In a culture that is high on subjectivism, in general, and experience, in particular, those of us in theological education must be the ones who will step back from personal involvement and present truthful, objective, and well-reasoned arguments on the issues involved.

At another level, intellectual proficiency is what is needed to respond to heresies within the Church and attacks from without. In many of our churches, emotionalism has been equated with true spirituality and reasoning with spiritual coldness. Additionally, experience has become the measure of most, if not all, things. Against this, we who pursue theological education must be the ones to correct heresies and provide the Biblical position.

This can only be used correctly if we are intellectually proficient. From outside the church come the attacks from the self-appointed philosophers of the day. Materialism, relativism, individualism, scepticism, and secular humanism have all been presented as the best way to go in this time. Where are the Christian thinkers of our day who are going to respond and chart a new course? Where will they come from? They must come from among us, from we who are involved in theological education. However, we can only accomplish this task if we are intellectually proficient.

APPENDIX 3

Secondly, theological education must make us ministerially competent. Ministerial competence speaks of effectively serving the needs of those in our churches and our communities. It means being able to listen to them and to answer their existential questions. Ministerial competence means more than just saying "Don't Worry" or "Jesus is the Answer." Ministerial competence means finding out what is the question. Yes, Jesus is the answer, but what is the question? *How* is Jesus the answer in their particular situation? Theological education must prepare us to answer that question. That which is gained in the classroom and in the library must be transferred to the churches, the classrooms and the counselling rooms in which we will serve.

When we leave an institution of learning we must be able to help the mother who has just seen her son gunned down and does not understand why. We must be able to say something to the woman in the ghetto who has six children for six different men and none is providing support. These things are all involved in ministerial competence for they all have to do with serving others. Our theological education must take us beyond the sheltered walls of the classroom and the library. If our theological education does not do that, then it needs to be re-thought. Our theological education must involve a theology of ministry.

Finally, theological education must make us spiritually eminent. Whereas intellectual proficiency has to do with our heads and ministerial competence has to do with our hands, spiritual eminence has to do with our hearts. Or, to change the analogy, whereas intellect relates to what we know and think, and ministry to what we do, spirituality has to do with who we are. There are many instances of people who developed full heads and empty hearts, or, to put it another way, hot heads and cold hearts. However, we are called to have cool heads and warm hearts. Spiritual eminence means that our theological education must draw us closer to God. It means that our relationship with God must deepen as our knowledge about Him increases. Spiritual eminence means that our knowledge about God must be translated into knowledge of God.

It is spiritual eminence that provides the love and power that is so vital for an effective ministry. It is spiritual eminence that will protect us from pride and arrogance, two of the theological students' most present temptations. If our theological education does not result in spiritual eminence, "education" it may be, but "theological education" it most certainly is not.

APPENDIX 4: GOD'S WILL

Distinction

WHAT SHOULD BE THE most important issue in your life and mine? The divine will. It is the will of God that Christians talk about the will of God (Eph. 5:24; Col. 3:16, 17). So we feel it fitting to confront you with the doctrine. Of course, it is more important to do God's will than to talk about it. That is why we shall discuss the matter of obedience to God's will later.

The importance of the will of God is seen in our Lord's life and teaching (Heb. 10: 5-7; Luke 22: 41-42; John 7:17). Probably the most crucial command for the believer is Ephesians 5:17; because if s/he truly obeys this injunction, s/he will be at least acquainted with the others. The will of the Lord should be made a matter of constant prayer (Luke 11:1-2; Col. 1:9; 4:12)

Description

In Romans 12:1-2, we see that the will of God is related to our dedication. It is described as "good and acceptable and perfect" in verse 2. The word "good" is sometimes used to describe God himself! As it relates to verse 2, the terms "useful, satisfactory, and beneficial" could make the description more meaningful for us. God's will is also acceptable.

This means that it is pleasing both to God and to us. As we shall try to show later, every aspect of God's will is perfect. Therefore, we should be careful how we talk about "God's perfect will," implying that sometimes there is an aspect that is less than perfect.

How do you feel after eating a good meal? It is a satisfying experience, isn't it? In John 4:31-34, the Lord seems to say exactly that. Doing God's will brings true and lasting satisfaction (1 John 2:17). God's will is always done in heaven. May we strive together to see it done here on earth (Matt. 6:10)

Definition

What is the will of God? It is said that for every complex question, there is a simple answer – and that answer is wrong!!! The answer to this question is somewhat involved but is of paramount importance.

There are (at least?) two aspects of the will of God: i) His decisions (or decrees; Dan 4:34-35; Eph. 1:3-5); ii)

His directions (eg., The law of Moses –OT; the law of Christ–NT, Gal. 6:2). It is the latter that is directly addressed to us. However, every Christian needs to be aware of the former. It is worthwhile noting that God's decisions are inscrutable. Not even the Apostle Paul fully understood them (Rom. 11:33). This is instructive.

Because of God's *decisions* we must pray, "Thy will be done" and we need to say, "God's willing" (James 4:13-15). Knowing God is sovereign should give us true poise (Rom. 8:28, Gen 50:20, Dan. 3:16-28). Though the *decisions* of God cannot be resisted (Dan 4:35), there is no injustice on God's part in their outworking (Rom 9:14, 19-20). And man is still free, though not absolutely.

It is the *directions* of God in the Bible, which are constantly resisted and disobeyed. Aren't we glad that there is an aspect of God's will that is irresistible? If this were not so, man would certainly turn the universe into a chaos.

According to Dr Charles C. Ryrie (*Balancing the Christian Life*, p.30), Israel had 613 commands (directions) to obey. He also says that there are hundreds of directions in the NT for believers today.

Do you want to know God's will? Our knowledge of God's will for the most part is in direct proportion to our knowledge of His *directions* (John 7:17).

Determination

To determine God's will for one's life means studying the Bible to discover His directions. The following outline, with God's guidance, may prove quite helpful.

Prayer: Am I earnestly seeking God's guidance? (Rom 1:10; Col. 1:9; 4:12).

Precept: Are there any commands, exhortations or prohibitions to obey? (Eph. 5:18).

Principles: Will I violate a scriptural guideline? (I Cor. 8:13; 10:31).

Precedents: Is there an example to follow or shun? (Phil 3:17; 1 Cor. 10: 1-13).

People: Am I seeking the advice of godly people, pastors, professors and parents, et al? (Prov. 11:14; Heb.13:17).

Promise: God's promises suggest a course of action (Study: Phil. 4:19 in context).

Preference: Am I making a wise choice based on the above? For example, "In 1 Cor. 7, several times Paul says that the will may choose among several *correct possibilities* (emphasis mine) so that any choice would be correct (vv. 36, 37, 39)." Charles C. Ryrie, *Balancing the Christian Life*, p. 47).

Demonstration

Our obedience to God's directives affords us the greatest opportunity to express our love to the Lord Jesus Christ (John 14:15). But doing God's will is never easy. One eminent seminary professor says that doing God's will is not difficult – it is impossible! He is right. In our own strength we are just like the Apostle Paul in Romans 7, (notice his frustration in verse 24).

APPENDIX 4

Fortunately for us we are not under law but under grace (Rom. 8:2-3). One of the major differences between law and grace is this: The law gave directions but no dynamic, but grace proffers both. (cf. Acts 15:10; John 1:16-18).

The dynamic of grace is the fullness of the Spirit. If Ephesians 5:17 is the most crucial verse for the Christian, then the following one (5:18) is the most powerful. God's will must be done in God's strength. Do you think Samson did God's will through mere muscles? If so, why were those muscles not evident to Delilah? (Notice her question: "Please tell us where your great strength is" Judges 16:6 NASB. It would seem to me that if Samson were very muscular, Delilah would not have asked such a question).

Samson's "muscles" were invisible (Judges 14:6; 16:20; 28, 29. Cf. Zech 4:6). Although our enemies are different, the source of our strength is the same (Eph 6: 10-18). And we become weak for the same reason – disobedience to God's directives (cf. Judges 16:17).

Discussion

In defining the will of God, what about His perfect and permissive will? And in determining God's will, what about providence and peace? The adjective "perfect" is used to describe God's directives both in Psalm 19:7 and Romans 12:2. So to be in God's perfect will is to be in obedience to God's perfect law (i.e. directives James 1:25).The term "permissive" is used by theologians to designate certain aspects of God's decrees which are inexplicable. For example, Acts 2:23 speaks about the crucifixion as being an outworking of God's decree. But it is equally clear from this verse that our Lord was murdered. This wicked act is said to be in God's permissive will.

Both peace and providence are unreliable means of ascertaining God's will. Of the former, Dr Dwight Pentecost writes: "...we must be careful if we have peace in doing a certain thing, because that peace may not be coming from the Spirit of God. The peace may come from the old nature that wanted to do that thing" (*Man's Problems God's Answers,* p. 164).But what about Colossians 3:15? "Peace may be defined negatively as the absence of anxiety within a person (as in Philippians, 4:6-7), or as the absence of hostility between persons. In Colossians 3:15, it is clearly the latter." (Gary Friessen, *Decision Making and the Will of God,* p. 142).

The same author puts the matter of providence in proper perspective, thus: "The only time that circumstances can be 'read' is when a divine interpretation is placed upon them by supernatural revelation. Apart from such revelation, circumstances may be taken to mean almost anything. . . Solomon made it clear that watching providence makes life seem futile (Ecclesiastes 1:1-11)." (Friesen, op. cit, p. 213.)

Documentation

Your will be done on earth as it is in heaven (Matt. 6:10 NIV). I have not sought happiness. I have sought to do the will of God and happiness has sought me. (E.S. Jones; cf. Ps. 23:6).

The will of God: nothing more, nothing less, nothing else (William Tyndale College) cf Heb 10:7.

Peace is the deliberate adjustment of my life to the will of God (Alan Redpath) cf. Phil. 4:6-7.

The Bible does not provide a map of life – only a compass. (H.W. Robinson) cf. Ps. 119:105.

Do God's will as if it is yours and He will do your will as if it were His (Gamaliel).

Whoever is willing to do what God wants will know whether what I teach comes from God or whether I speak on my own authority. (John 7:17 – Good News Bible).

Mining the Scriptures

Proverbs 2:1-6: Look for these nuggets: The will/wisdom of God: anything He:

- Prizes (Gold) — Ex 34:18, 19; Jn 1: 14
- Prescribes — Eph. 5:18; 1 Thess. 5:16
- Proscribes — (Rom. 12:17, 19)
- Promotes — 1 Cor 9:1-27*Promotes (Silver)
- Promises — 1 Jn 1:9
- Provides — 1 Cor. 10:1-14
- Permits (Diamonds) —Rom. 15: 20, 22-29*

APPENDIX 5
THE JNT AND ACTS

IN THIS COMMENTARY, we have included excerpts from the JNT, because language is near the heart of every culture. And once again the Bible Society of the West Indies has made its clearest intention to translate the entire Bible into the Jamaican language commonly called Patwa, Jamaican Creole, or simply, Jamaican. The announcement has sparked a heated discussion in the form of a flurry of letters to the editors of our leading print media.

Most of the responses express the view that the project is ill-conceived, and, if carried through, will be a colossal waste of time and money. One seemingly strong argument for the continued marginalization of the Jamaican language is the ubiquitous character of English and the contrasting narrow confines of Patwa.

A few writers, mostly academicians,[307] have come out in support of the idea, pointing out that a possible reason for the poor performance of many of our young people in their English examinations is the failure of the education

APPENDIX 5

system to recognize Jamaican Creole as the mother tongue of the majority. They also point out that in other countries like Haiti and the ABC islands, where the languages of the majority are duly recognized, the learning of French and Dutch, colonial languages like English, is made far easier.

Some prominent individuals who have spoken or written on what is now becoming the Patwa-English impasse include former Prime Minister the honourable Mr. Bruce Golding. He is a representative of those who strongly feel that the promotion of the Jamaican language at this time may be counter-productive to the proper grasp of English, the official language since independence. But perhaps the most worthwhile contribution to the debate so far is that of the Honorary Consul for the Federation of St. Kitts-Nevis to the Republic of South Africa and lecturer at the University of KwaZulu-Natal, Dr Gosnell L. Yorke.

Dr Yorke spent over fifteen years in Africa, and was for ten years a Bible translation consultant with the United Bible Societies. In a recent Gleaner article, Dr Yorke informs us that our region is witnessing what he calls a linguistic phenomenon in that the four European languages that were imperially imposed on our African ancestors are now undergoing a process of "creolisation." What he means by this is that the early slave settlers of Jamaica, for example, "were forced to creatively adapt" the language of their European overlords, and their adaptation blended with the various west African languages to produce before long a new authentic language we now call Jamaican Creole . Professor York went on to say that:

Since the various Bible translation agencies in the Caribbean are driven by the defensible conviction that all 6,000 or so languages currently spoken in the world at large are equal, that English is only one of them, and that God does speak most compellingly to each of us in our mother tongue or heart language . . . it is not at all surprising that the Haitian Bible Society, the Bible Society of The Netherlands Antilles, and the Bible Society in the Eastern Caribbean have already translated and published . . . the complete Bible or at least the New Testament in some of the Caribbean creoles.[308]

We are informed as well that ongoing translation work is also going on in Belize and the French Antilles—and, further afield, in many parts of Africa. A few contributors to the debate, some as far as Canada and the USA, who are largely in disagreement with the likes of Dr Yorke, appear to say that Jamaica Creole only has entertainment value. For instance, where else in the world do they go to a shop and order *wan drinks and two patti*! Or where on earth do competent speakers of their mother tongue drop their aches at *Arba* Street and pick it up at *Heast* Street? The present attitude toward the Jamaican language is strikingly similar to that toward English in the Middle Ages. Thus Alister *McGrath* could write:

It is not generally realized that the languages of the elite in English society in the early fourteenth century were French and Latin. English was seen as the language of the peasants, incapable of expressing anything other than the crudest and most basic of matters. . . . How could such a barbaric language do justice to such sophisticated matters

APPENDIX 5

as philosophy or religion? To translate the Bible from its noble and ancient languages into English was seen as a pointless act of debasement.[309]

In this regard, a Jamaican proverb comes readily to mind: *ol'time sinting cum bac hagain*! Or in the language of King Solomon, "There is nothing new under the sun." Again we cite professor Yorke's insightful comments on the matter:

After all, Jesus himself is known to have spoken Aramaic, his own mother tongue, and not only Hebrew, the language of the Jewish Scriptures but (and if He did at all) also the two dominant languages of his day, namely, the commonly-spoken Greek which was made possible by the colonial exploits and exploitation of Alexander, the Great, who lived and died before His time or Latin, the official language of the conquering Romans-those who ruled the world when He both lived and died; when He uttered His life-changing words and performed His life-changing works. And if Jesus showed no hesitation in embracing Aramaic, His mother tongue, in His conduct and conversation with others around Him, including when dying on the cross, then why should one hesitate do so in Jamaican-if that just happens to be one's mother tongue?

In John 3:7 this same Jesus is reported to have said to Nicodemus: Marvel not that I said unto thee, ye must be born again. This, of course, is the King James translation of a fairly well-known text. What apparently is not fairly well known is that modern English has not really improved on this rendition due to the fact that its pronominal system is sometimes quite vague, especially in the second person.

Therefore, one finds the same verse translated in the New International Version (NIV) as: "You should not be surprised at my saying, "You must be born again."" In the King James language of over 400 years ago the distinction between 'you' singular and 'you' plural is clearly marked by the pronouns 'thee' and 'ye' respectively; but in the NIV there is no such clarity, except for a footnote to the effect that the second occurrence of the pronoun in question is plural.

This is not the fault of the NIV translators; it is the weakness of the Queen's English in modern dress. Other Europeans languages such as German, French and Spanish, can make the distinction and so bring a better understanding to the verse. There is still another language that says it better than modern English: *So no fraitn wen yu ier mi tel yu se, 'Unu afi baan wan neks taim!'*[310]

The same insight can be gained from passages like Genesis 3:1 and Luke 22:31where the word 'you' is also plural and where the Jamaican *unu* would make better sense than its official counterpart. We therefore cannot wait to see what other insights the full Jamaican Bible will bring. In the meantime, we will continue to make much use of this delicate language.

---

[307] See especially E. Christine Campbell in the Bibliography.
[308]'Patois Bible in Pan-African and Pan-Caribbean Context.' http://jamaica-gleaner.com/gleaner/20080629/lead/lead8.html.

APPENDIX 5

[309] *The Story of the King James Bible and How it Changed a Nation, a Language, and a Culture* (New York: Doubleday, 2001), 24.

[310] *Di Jamiekan Nyuu Testiment* (Kingston: Bible Society of the West Indies, 2012); *wan neks taim*, i.e., 'from above.'

APPENDIX 6

Sabbath, Sunday, and the Third-Millennium Saint

A VERY STRANGE situation exists among Christians today. All Christians worship the same God; they all have the very same Jesus as saviour. All Christians accept essentially the same Bible. Yet they have two days of worship! On one hand there is a large group of sincere Christians, who tell us, "Sunday is the Christian day of worship!" Another equally sincere group replies, "no, Saturday, the seventh day, is the day on which Christians should worship!" How can we decide the question? The only way to know religious truth is to go to God's word. It does not matter what a church may teach or what a preacher may preach; the only really important question is: "What does God say in the Bible?"

APPENDIX 6

The paragraph above forms the introduction to a pamphlet entitled, "How Sunday Keeping Started." The purpose of the pamphlet is to demonstrate that the day of worship was never divinely changed from Saturday to Sunday.[311] The author of the pamphlet first discusses eight occurrences of the phrase "first day of the week" and convincingly shows that none of these texts authorizes such a change. The references are Matthew 28:1; Mark 16:1,2; Mark 16:9; Luke 24:1; John 20:1; and 1 Corinthians 16:1,2.

The writer then argues that the term "Lords day" found in Revelation 1:10 is not a reference to the first day of the week. Based on Matthew 12:8, s/he concludes that the "Lord's day" is Saturday. "How then did Sunday observance come into the Church?" s/he asks. Taking a cue from Daniel 7:25, the writer answers the question: "It came about as a direct result of Satan's attempts to counterfeit God's work." Later on, the Roman Catholic Church is clearly identified as the group which "took the lead among Christians in attempting to change the weekly day to Sunday."

I am in agreement with the pamphlet on a couple of matters. First, I thoroughly endorse the statement which affirms that the only thing that matters on the question of the Sabbath is what God says in His Word. I also agree that there is no text in the Bible that mentions any change of the Sabbath from Saturday to Sunday.

However, to insist that Christians keep the Sabbath today is entirely a different matter. While it is true that the idea of the Sabbath is as old as creation (Gen. 2:2-3), it is to be carefully noted that the command to keep the Sabbath was given only to the Israelites (Ex 31:12-17). In Psalm 147:19-20 the Psalmist celebrates the fact that God's law was received by his people alone. He concludes by saying, "He hath not dealt so with any nation; as for his judgements they have not known them." In other words, the Egyptians, Babylonians, and other nearby peoples did not have the written word of God.

Therefore, those surrounding nations were not required to worship on a Saturday. The same is true today. If, however, an outsider wanted to enter into covenant relationship with the God of the Israelites, that person would have had to accept the Mosaic stipulations as well.

When we come to the New Testament, we find the Lord Jesus Christ keeping the Sabbath as an obedient Jew. The Apostle Paul also visited the synagogues on the Sabbath. Was he merely keeping the Sabbath as a good Christian? Before this question is answered, let us examine two passages from his writings.

Colossians 2:13-15

In this portion the apostle carefully points out some of the accomplishments of Christ on the cross. These include:
1. Remission of sins and their consequence (v. 13)
2. Cancellation of Sinai and its Covenant (v.14)
3. Spoliation of Satan and his cohorts (v. 15)

APPENDIX 6

Based on these achievements the apostle warns: "Allow no one, therefore, to take you to task [or criticize you] about what you eat or drink or over the observance of a festival, new moon, or Sabbath" (v. 16, REB).[312]

In light of the above, the following question should be pondered: why is the Sabbath imperative conspicuously absent from the New Testament? I am quite sure that Sabbatarians have an answer to this query, but I find it difficult to see how they can avoid its implication for the believer today.[313]

Romans 14:5-7

Although the Apostle Paul recognized that the Old Testament law was not binding on believers in his day (Rom. 6:14, cf. Heb. 7:12), he nevertheless allowed for the observance of any day a Christian may have wished to set apart. Thus, he writes, "One man considers one day more sacred than another; another man should be fully convinced in his own mind. He who regards one day special does so to the Lord" (Rom 14:5-6a; REB).

So, is Sunday the Christian Sabbath? Certainly not. However, since Christians have been delivered from the Mosaic Law (Rom. 7:1-6), they now serve God "in newness of spirit, and in the oldness of the letter." This allows freedom to worship on any appropriate day. Knowing this, the early Christians settled into a pattern of Sunday worship. It would appear that it was these same believers who dubbed the first day of the week "the Lord's day" (Rev

1:10), most likely because of its association with the resurrection of Christ (Matt 28), his subsequent Sunday appearances (John 20:19, 26), and the advent of the Spirit on the first day of the week.[314] This may be confirmed by other early Christian writings.[315]

Why then did the Apostle Paul visit the synagogues on the Sabbath? Without a doubt, he was carrying out the very principle he wrote about in 1 Corinthians 9:19-21. He wanted to evangelize his fellow Jews. Of particular interest here is the Apostle's testimony regarding his relationship with the Old Testament law on the one hand and its New Testament counterpart on the other. "To Jews I behave like a Jew, to win the Jews, that is, to win those under the law I behave as if under the law, though not myself subject to the law (v. 20, REB)."

Those who are under the law according to this verse are the Jewish people. The Apostle Paul himself was a Jew. Yet, writing as a Christian missionary, he categorically declares that "I

myself [am] not subject to the law" Amazing! But does this mean that the Apostle to the Gentiles was lawless? God forbid! The cowboy from the Wild West could have shouted "hallelujah"! I'm no longer under the law; I'm an outlaw," but he would not have had any support from Paul's letters. Some first-century believers may have thought along those lines but this kind of thinking was seriously challenged (cf. Rom. 6:14-23; Gal 4:21-5:1).

There was a time when a certain Saul of Tarsus took pride in being under the Mosaic Law (Phil. 3:5-10). But the Christ event made a gigantic difference in his life, so

APPENDIX 6

much so that his new ground of boasting was in the Messianic code (1 Cor 9:21; "under law to Christ") and the Messianic cross, which forms its basis (Gal. 6:14). So must the twenty-first century saint keep the Sabbath? S/he may if s/he wishes. But if s/he mandates this for everybody s/he would, I believe, be guilty of putting a yoke on the necks of God's people which many are unable to bear.

---

[311] Another tract, entitled "The Mark of the Beast," goes a step further by identifying Sunday observance as the mark of the beast.

[312] In the following verse the Apostle points out, with some literary flourish, that the Sabbath (along with rites mentioned in v. 16) is a shadow (*skia*), the substance (*soma*) of which is Christ.

[313] Especially in the light of the fact that in Col 2 the nearest (though not exclusive) antecedent of "which" (AV; v. 17) or "these" (NIV) is the Sabbath.

[314] This can be inferred from the "7 weeks since Passover that had been fulfilled." (F.F. Bruce, *The Acts of the Apostles*. London: Tyndale, 1951, p. 81).

[315] For example, in *the Didache*, xiv. 1, the term rendered "Lord's" (*Kuriake*) in Revelation 1:10 is used for Sunday. "After having assembled and confessed your transgressions break the bread [and] give thanks on

The Dominical day (*kuriaken*) of the Lord." G.P Gould (ed.), *The Apostolic Fathers* vol. 1 (Cambridge, M.A: Harvard, 1912), 330. "The phrase [the Lord's day] is clearly and consistently used of Sunday from the second half of the second century on,"G. K. Beale, *The Book of Revelation* (Grand Rapids: Eerdmans, 1999), 203. Even the SDA scholar, S. Bacchiocchi, (*From Sabbath to Sunday* [Rome: PGU, 1977], 123-30) rejects the Lord's day=Sabbath view. Unfortunately, though, he opts for the equally untenable eschatological day of the Lord.

APPENDIX 7

PENTECOST AND THE BRIDE

THIS YEAR THE ISLES of Cyprus and Jamaica (and many other countries around the globe) celebrate the Feast of Weeks popularly known as the Day of Pentecost. Cyprus, unlike JA, dates back to Bible times and came into prominence during the reign of King David in the tenth century BC.

During the Christian era their most famous son of the soil is one 'Bar-Nabbas' Joseph who was nicknamed the Counsellor par excellence. The word Pentecost (fiftieth day) is derived from one of the two national languages of Cyprus. This is how the term Pentecost is used in the so-called Maccabee Bible, because the festival was celebrated fifty days after the Passover celebrations.

It is also well known that the Jewish Scriptures were written in the Hebrew language, but what is not apparently well known is that the Jews themselves were the first ones to translate the Hebrew Bible into Greek, while they were living in Africa. The translation was done over two hundred years before the birth of Christ and is still being used to this day. It is this version, popularly known as the Septuagint (LXX), that first associated the term Pentecost with the feast mentioned in Leviticus 23:16. A literal rendering of this text reads "you shall number pentekonta days"; here the verb 'number' is related to our English word 'arithmetic' and of course the numerical adjective pentekonta is the term for fifty.

In Second Maccabees 12 we have an interesting account of a Jewish battle against their enemies. In verse 31 we read about what happened before this skirmish: "and so they came to Jerusalem, to the feast of weeks," and we also read in the following verse "And after . . . Pentecost they went . . . against . . . the governor of Idumea."

The verses are interesting because they give us two of the names of this great Jewish festival—the one preferred by Jews themselves living in and around Jerusalem and the other which became popular among the people of God living in the diaspora, that is, the *Hag Shavuot* or feast of weeks found in, Deuteronomy 16:10.

The term feast of weeks refers primarily to the seven weeks or forty-nine days between the Jewish Passover and the fiftieth day of special celebration that normally falls on a Sunday. The same event is also called the feast of first fruits, because Pentecost was originally a harvest festival.

For a number of Orthodox Jews it is still commemorated as such. Whereas it is a one day celebration for Jews today, the Orthodox Christians on the island of Cyrus do so over three days. Day one is dubbed Trinity Sunday, day two, Spirit Monday, and the Tuesday, the Day of the Trinity.

Christianity in the west for the most part seldom highlights Pentecost, the day the church became the bride of Christ. But what has left an indelible mark on the West is the spiritual awakening of the early twentieth century known has the Pentecostal movement. The movement itself is heavily indebted to Luke's account of the coming of the Spirit recorded in Acts 2.

While Pentecostal Christians cannot claim all the credit for the fifty-percent of Jamaicans who testify that the Spirit of God is living in them, it would be foolhardy and unkind to ignore their contribution to this aspect of authentic nation building; for without it, there shall no flesh be saved alive! We thank God, then, for the first Christian Pentecost and the harvest of souls then and now, as well as the three thousand one hundred and twenty who received the Spirit on that memorable day. Shalom.

APPENDIX 8

A Birthday Worth Celebrating
[Dr David Corbin]

UNLIKE CHRISTMAS, THE BIRTHDAY of the church gets little visibility in most churches. That is so unfortunate, considering the church was birthed on a celebrative day, an occasion that brought together thousands of Jews for the Feast of Weeks.

he Feast of Weeks is the second of the three "solemn feasts" that all Jewish males were required to travel to Jerusalem to attend. To the Jews, this time of celebration is known as Shavuot, which is the Hebrew word meaning "weeks." Shavuot marked the beginning of the new agricultural season.

Shavuot was a joyous time of giving thanks and presenting offerings for the new grain of summer wheat harvest. At times Shavuot was called the Feast of Harvest and the Feast of First Fruit. Whereas these titles reflect the agricultural nature of the celebration, the Feast of Weeks addressed the timing of the festive celebration.

The celebration started seven full weeks, or exactly fifty days, after Passover. In the Old Testament, we read where God commanded the Jews to count seven full weeks (49 days), beginning on the second day of Passover (Leviticus 23:15-16). For this reason, some refer to this festival as the Feast of the Fiftieth Day - from the Greek word *pentecostes*, meaning fiftieth. This is the same day referred to as the Day of Pentecost in the New Testament.

According to the New Testament, it was on the Day of Pentecost that the church was launched (Acts 2). Thousands of Jews were in Jerusalem to celebrate the start of another agricultural season. They approached that festival with thoughts of a new harvest, new beginnings and new hope. No one expected that that year's festival would be unique. That festival, fifty days following the death of Jesus, coincided with the promise of Jesus – "do not leave Jerusalem, but wait for the gift my Father promised...".

Acts 2:1 begins with the words, "when the day of Pentecost came...". That simple statement is loaded with history and expectation. That was to be an occasion of thanksgiving and acknowledging God's provision. An occasion when non-Jews could celebrate with Jews.

That was the context in which the church was launched. On that day of Pentecost, the Holy Spirit empowered simple fishermen from Galilee to speak in languages they did not know. On that day more than 3,000 persons were converted to a new faith, affirming that Jesus of Nazareth was the promised Messiah. On that day the prophecy of Joel was partially fulfilled – "I will pour out my Spirit on all people..."

This weekend marks the anniversary of that festival. While Jews are celebrating Shavuot, some Christians are

APPENDIX 8

celebrating Pentecost. Sunday, May 20 is referred to as Pentecost Sunday. Some churches in Europe talk about Whit Sunday, from an old English idea of wearing white on that day. Both Jews and Christians celebrate the day, fifty days after Passover.

According to the Jewish Talmud, it was on that day, the Law was given to Moses. So, as Jews celebrate Shavuot this weekend, they will read portions from the Book of Ruth. They will be reminded of the Law that provides for the non-Jew, as in the case of Ruth. Some will gather at late-night study sessions to commemorate the giving of the Torah.

Christians on the other hand, will remember the birthday of the Church. Christians will remember the coming of the promised Holy Spirit. More liturgical churches observe this day annually on the seventh Sunday after Easter. Pentecostal churches within evangelical traditions also celebrate Pentecost Sunday.

Although my local church does not traditionally observe Pentecost Sunday, I intend to use the time to reflect on the rich harvest of converts at the launching of the church. I hope to reflect on the promise of the prophet Joel concerning God's desire "to pour out His Spirit" on all ethnic communities. Pentecost Sunday is a great time to revisit our attitude to immigration; wouldn't this be a wonderful opportunity to reach out to persons who are ethnically different from us?

More than anything else, this would be a great opportunity to experience the control of the Holy Spirit in our lives. Try to imagine a world with Spirit-controlled persons, infiltrating our communities with "love, joy, peace, patience, kindness, goodness, faithfulness, gentleness and self-control" (Galatians 5:22-23).

APPENDIX 9

Prima Inter Partes? Prisca as Pastor and the People of God

THIS PAPER JOINS RECENT researchers (Keller 2014; cf. Smart 2012) in investigating the probability that there were female leaders in the earliest church. It begins with a poem summarizing the traditional position and proceeds to make a modest case against it by examining some of the scriptural pillars on which it is grounded, bearing in mind the hermeneutical challenge and caveat posed by a leading advocate of Caribbean Theology and gender inclusiveness: "A Gospel entrapped in Third World prejudiced interpretations is no better than one entrapped in Western inconsistencies, betrayals, and speculations" (Boothe 1996, 21). Now for the poem (Hall 2011, 210):

> Women in the Church
> Have their special role
> Equal in salvation

But not to have control

Preaching is forbidden
And so is pastoral rule
But apart from those restrictions
Everything is cool

This doesn't mean we are inferior,
Less intelligent, gifted or weak
It simply means what it says
We are not to rule or speak

We are called to function
Each, in a peculiar way
To Minister with our spiritual gift
For which we are the perfect fit

Therefore, we implore you sister
There is much scope to serve
For needs are always many
And hands are always few
Just waiting dear sister
For God to hear from you

APPENDIX 9

INTRODUCTION

I believe the traditional position on female leadership in church can only be strengthened, modified or overturned by listening/reading to a robust presentation of an alternative reading (e.g., Howe 1982) of the main biblical texts on which it is based. Unfortunately, this paper is definitely not rigorous enough to meet the demands of such a work. What it does attempt to do, however, is to provide basic bibliographical leads (see Works Cited) within the context of my own survey of what is considered to be a better approach to the question.

We may begin with the founding of the church in Acts 2. When the Spirit came at Pentecost in fulfillment of the Founder's promise (Acts 1: 5; cf. 11: 15-17), one hundred and twenty believers were awaiting his arrival in an upper room--both sisters and brothers (Acts 1: 12-14).

These were not only the embryonic members of the soon-to-be-formed body of Christ; they were in a real sense the first leaders of that entity. At the very least this was true of the men (Peter, 'solid as a rock', et al). All were intimately related to the ascended Lord and were uniquely equipped to teach the 3000 people who became believers (Acts 2: 42). It is difficult to imagine only the men teaching the new converts in the several house churches in and around Jerusalem (Liefeld 1990, 31).

In support of the above, Peter's citation of Joel 2 regarding God's Spirit being poured out on all flesh is saying, among other things, that leadership among the people of God will no longer be confined to male prophets, priests, kings but upon potential 'prophetesses' (Jewish tradition recognizes seven prophetesses: Sarah, Miriam, Deborah, Hannah, Abigail, Huldah and Esther! [Rabbi Scherman 1998, 2038]), and 'priestesses' as well (Acts 2: 16-18; cf. Rev. 1:6). So we are not surprised to find within the pages of Acts a wife and husband team engaged in the exposition of sacred scripture:

An im [Apollos] neva fried, so im staat fi taak chrang chrang iina di Juu dem choch, bot wen Prisila an Akwila ier im, dem tek im wan said an tiich im so im kuda andastan Gad wod beta. (Acts 18:26; JNT).

He [Apollos] began to speak boldly in the synagogue. When Priscilla and Aquila heard him, they invited him to their home and explained to him the way of God more adequately (Acts 18:26; NIV).

Romans, the book following Acts, further informs us that this wife and husband team had a church in their house (Rom. 16: 3-5: 'Greet also the church that meets at their house'-v. 5. Note the order 'Prisca and Aquila' in Rom.16: 3 and Acts 18: 27. The expected word order for a union of this nature is found in 1 Cor. 16: 19). Bearing in mind Acts 18:26, that Priscilla and Aquila were not merely hosting the people of God on a week-end; they were actually providing leadership to the nascent church, particularly in the area of the exposition of Old Testament scripture (cf. Acts 2:42; 2 Tim. 3:16-17). 1 Cor. 16:19 makes a similar point: '. . . Aquila and Prisca send their best wishes in the Lord, together with the church that meets in their house'(NJB;my emphasis). In this context, the mention of children in 1 Timothy 3:4 makes better sense, since the household is the church on Sundays (cf. 1 Cor. 16:2).

THE CONGREGANTS OF EPHESUS AND THE LEADERSHIP QUESTION
Ephesians 4

'The church of Ephesus is perhaps the most fortunate in the New Testament in that it is somehow associated with seven inspired epistles . . . Ephesians . . . 1 Timothy . . . 2 Timothy, 1 John, 2 John, [and] 3 John. . . .', and the last in Revelation 2 (*Quest* 2002, 21-22; cf. Hultgren 2003, 150). What is the relevance of all this? At least three of these letters make a contribution to our understanding of what church leadership was like in the first century.

In Ephesians 4, for example, we are informed that when Christ ascended he gave gifts to 'people' (v. 8; NRSV). The term translated 'men' in King James as well as the New International Version is a generic one and has reference to both genders. The linguistic phenomenon of using a masculine plural term to include both sexes is common to the two main languages of the Bible. For instance, most of the references to 'children of Israel' in the Old Testament are literally 'sons of Israel'. The same is true of passages like Romans 8:14, Galatians 3:7, 26; 4:6; 1 Thessalonians 5:5, and Hebrews 12:8.

So all the gifted individuals mentioned in Ephesians 4:11 are to be understood as male and female leaders who function according to the ' grace . . . [and] the measure of the gift of Christ.' (v.7). It is clear from the context that these sisters and brothers alluded to in verse 11 are exercising leadership, or better, are expected to carry out leadership functions, because verses 12 and 13 in particular lead to such a conclusion: 'to prepare God's people for works of service, so that the body of Christ may be built up until we all reach unity in the faith and in the knowledge of the Son of God and become mature, attaining to the whole measure of the fullness of Christ' (NIV; italics added).

If, as we are positing, the gifts of Ephesians 4:11 are special leadership endowments, how do they differ from other lists, and how do believers with similar endowments function within or without the corpus Christi? In order to formulate an answer, some important distinctions must be made. If, for example, the gift of evangelism enables a sister/brother to effectively witness to unbelievers, it is still the privilege of every believer to witness. But the brother/sister with this gift has the additional responsibility of training or equipping members of the body to do evangelism. The same line of reasoning applies to the gifts of teaching, church planting (apostles), pastoring, and prophesying. To adapt a truism from education: these gifted individuals not only give a fish to be eaten for a day; they equip others to do fishing so that they may eat for a lifetime. This is an essential part of Christian leadership within the local church, since 'Equipping the Saints is the purpose, task and responsibility of the Church leaders' (Roper 1999, 55). Thus we hear from one first century leader to another first century leader (ministering in Ephesus):

And the things you have heard me say in the presence of many witnesses entrust to reliable men who will also be qualified to teach others (2 Tim. 2: 2; NIV).

Bearing in mind the nature of our study, we will now focus our attention on only two of the gifts mentioned in Ephesians 4:11, that of the apostle and that of the pastor/teacher. If we are correct in coming to the conclusion that all the gifts in this verse are special leadership gifts and that none of them is limited to a particular gender within the body of Christ, then the further conclusion is escapable: Christ has also given to his church female apostles and pastors 'to prepare God's people for works of service, so that the body of Christ may be built up' (v. 12). To have it any other way is to short circuit the divinely intended process of edification, and so impoverish the body. We have already seen from Acts 18 and Romans 16 that Prisca was carrying out a pastoral role in her house-church, along with her husband. In the same chapter of Romans (v. 7) we have another prominent sister (Junia) being classed among the apostles:

Greet Andronicus and Junia, my relatives who were in prison with me; they are prominent among the apostles, and they were in Christ before I was (NRSV).

The verse presents two pertinent exegetical problems. The first has to do with the gender of 'Junia/s'. The NIV ('Greet Andronicus and Junias . . . .') construes the original as masculine (contra the NRSV above), and at least one commentator believes 'It is impossible to know for sure if the second of the names is the feminine . . . .' (Kroll 2002, 239). Notwithstanding this level of skepticism, the evidence for taking the original term as feminine is getting stronger by the hour, because whereas Junia was a common first century name,[316] Junias is still unattested (Osborne 2004, 406-407; Schreiner 2001, 400; see also Lampe 1991, 222-224).

The next problem surrounds the phrase 'prominent among the apostles' (KJV: 'who are of note among the apostles'). Does it mean that Andronicus and Junia were well known by those within the apostolic circle or that they themselves were outstanding apostles? Our answer in part depends on our definition of 'apostles'. In the New Testament there are at least two classes of apostles are delineated: those that belonged to the original band (Acts 1: 12-26; cf. 1 Cor. 15:9) and those who possess the gift (1 Cor. 12: 29a). Based on the criteria of Acts 1, Barnabas has to be placed in this latter grouping (Acts 14: 14). And if we understand 'prominent among the apostles'[317] in an inclusive way (like Johnson 2001, 233-234; and others)[318], Junia[319] is also similarly positioned—and, of course, the other female apostles of Ephesians 4:11.

The other key term of Ephesians 4: 11 is that of the pastor/teacher, one of 'the main offices' emphasized by the writer (Black 2002, 128). Black (2002, 130) rightly points out that the one definite article governing both 'pastors and teachers' strongly suggests that one office is view. This is done, presumably, to underscore the main function of the church leader, that of teaching (cf. Acts 20: 27-30).

If we treat the two terms separately or together, there is just nothing within the context that says that any of these gifts is limited to a certain segment of the priesthood (cf. Rev. 1:5b-6). If the inspired writer had wanted to, he would have most certainly made it clear that only brothers, and not sisters, can occupy the office of the pastor.

First Timothy 3

This is the most discussed passage in the world today. Interpretations range from seeing Paul as a liberator and champion of women's rights to dismissing Paul as wrong and irrelevant in today's culture. George Bernard Shaw even called Paul, the "eternal enemy of women" (Mounce 2000, 103).

Regarding the qualifications of 1 Tim. 3, we need to bear in mind that it is natural for the language to be couched in such a way as to give the impression that only males can become church leaders, because of the nature of the common form of communication of the day. So, similar to the point made above regarding terms such as 'pastors' and 'apostles', a word like 'Brethren/brothers' actually means 'sisters and brothers' (e.g. 1Cor. 10:1; Rom. 12:1).[320] The same is true of the key pronoun of 1 Timothy 3: 1. The Authorized Version, both in its 'ancient' (17th cent.) and modern (20th; i.e., the New King James) forms, renders this indefinite pronoun (*tis*) as 'man'. Of course, such a translation can be understood in a generic sense, but, especially in this passage, it can be misleading.

Other English Versions, therefore, have 'anyone' (NIV) or 'whoever' (NRSV; cf. Louw and Nida 1989, 814-815) instead. A partial survey of the usage of this pronoun in the Pauline literature may be useful (the occurrences cited below are in bold type and are taken from KJV):

For scarcely for a righteous man will one die: yet peradventure for a good man some [one] would even dare to die (Rom. 5:7).

But ye are not in the flesh, but in the Spirit, if so be that the Spirit of God dwell in you. Now if any man have not the Spirit of Christ, he is none of his (Rom. 8:9).

Lest any [one] should say that I had baptized in mine own name (1 Cor. 1:15).

For while one saith, I am of Paul; and another, I *am* **of Apollos; are ye not carnal? (1Cor. 3:4).**

Now if any man build upon this foundation gold, silver, precious stones, wood, hay, stubble. . . (1 Cor. 3:12).

If any man defile the temple of God, him shall God destroy; for the temple of God is holy, which *temple* **ye are. Let no man deceive himself. If any man among you**

seemeth to be wise in this world, let him become a fool, that he may be wise (1 Cor. 3:17, 18).

Moreover, it is required in stewards, that a man be found faithful (1 Cor. 4:2).

But now I have written unto you not to keep company, if any man that is called a[ny] brother/[sister][321] be a fornicator, or covetous, or an idolater, or a railer, or a drunkard, or an extortioner; with such an one no not to eat (1 Cor. 5:11).

Dare any of you, having a matter against another, go to law before the unjust, and not before the saints? (1 Cor. 6: 1).

And if any man think that he knoweth any thing, he knoweth nothing yet as he ought to know. But if any man love God, the same is known of him (1 Cor. 8:2, 3).

But we know that the law *is* good, if a man use it lawfully (1 Tim. 1:8).

Whenever this pronoun is employed it is invariably a reference to 'someone' without any regard to gender, unless it governs a noun that is gender specific (Louw & Nida 1989, 814-815).[322] An example from 1Timothy may be cited:

If any woman who is a believer has widows in her family, she should help them and not let the church be burdened with them, so that the church can help those widows who are really in need (5:16).[323]

The point of this survey is to lay emphasis on the apostle's opening statement of 1 Timothy 3:1: 'Here is a trustworthy saying: If *anyone* sets his [or 'her'] heart on being an overseer, [s/]he desires a noble task.' Writing today in our gender inclusive culture, Paul, I believe, would have written just a sentence.

But what about chapter 2 of First Timothy, which appears to strictly prohibit a woman from teaching or having authority over the man? As is pointed out (e.g. Fee 1988, 72-79[324]), this prohibition against women (better, 'wives' in my view) addresses a situation of heresy at the time-- underscoring the need to remind ourselves of the occasional nature of the letter.[325] In other words, if both wife and husband are co-pastors (Aquila and Priscilla or Junia and her husband), there is no need for one or the other to 'usurp authority',[326] which, apparently, some of the Ephesian wives were doing. The principle is applicable to both genders, just as 1 Tim. 5: 6 would apply as well to a widower.[327]

1 Timothy 2: 8-15 is the paragraph in the New Testament which provides the injunctions. . . most cited as conclusive by those who oppose preaching, teaching, and leadership ministries for women in the church.[328] It is inappropriate, however, to isolate verses 11-12 from the immediate context of 1 Timothy 2: 8-15. If any paragraph is perceived as culturally bound (as 2:8-10 often is) or especially difficult in terms of Pauline Theology (as 2: 15[329] often is), it must realized that these same issues must be confronted in understanding 2:11-14 (Scholer 1985, 7; see also Tee 2002, 1-42, 105-122).

APPENDIX 9

2 John

The final Ephesian[330] (house) church we will look at is the one addressed in the epistle of 2 John. 'John addresses this short letter to "the chosen lady" (and her children), whom some take to be a woman who allowed a church to meet in her house and others take to be a personification of a particular church' (Elwell and Yarbrough 1998, 369). The perspective that is deemed to be the correct one here is that the letter is addressed to 'a woman who allowed a church to meet in her house.'[331] In the wider context of epistolary literature, every letter written to an individual (such as Timothy or Titus or Philemon) presupposes a literal person. The main difficulty here is that the person is a woman. So it would appear that many Bible students prefer to 'allegorize' her.

Such an allegorical or metaphorical approach also eliminates the question as to what role does this woman play in the church she houses. If Paul, when addressing a 1st Timothy or his 'brother', 2nd Timothy (or Titus or Philemon) is writing to a church leader (and by extension his church), why is it that the apostle John is writing only to a 'congregation' (Westermann 1969, 159), and not to a church leader, as he does to Gaius (3 John)?

It is Spencer (1985, 109-111) who has provided the most compelling argument at this juncture for taking the 'The elect lady' as a duly elected church official. She points out that the term translated 'lady'[332] is the feminine of 'lord' or 'master', and, like its grammatically masculine counterpart, 'lady' (especially in this context) represents an authority figure. 'Consequently, the children are "hers," just as the children of 1 John are "his" (John's). . . Moreover, in the last verse John indicates that there was another such woman who also was an overseer over a church community.'

Admittedly, 2 John provides the weakest argument for female leadership in the early church, but, if accepted, it is a part of the cumulative evidence presented earlier.

Conclusion

We have presented a case for seeing within the pages of the New Testament a phenomenon that is seldom examined—that veiled within the language of grammatically plural nouns, such as 'apostles' and 'pastors', is the stark reality of female church leaders. The case is strongest, we believe, in Ephesians 4 and meets its stiffest challenge in First Timothy 2. But once the two letters are interpreted within their own occasional contexts (the former less so than the latter), the tension between the two is greatly minimized. This relatively new way of looking at ancient Scripture, it is hoped, may aid in the cause of inter-denominational and intra- denominational justice issues, especially as they relate to the employment of ecclesiastical power, for, by and large:

> Justice as equality calls for the dismantling of all relationships of oppression and domination, which result when

the fundamental equality of all human beings [Gen 1:26-28; Gal 3:28] is disregarded. In so doing, it takes account of the multiple dimensions of the human person (social, spiritual, material) and calls a society just when it allows for the flourishing of every member, specifically through full participation in the life of the society [and church?] (Perkins, 2013, 167; emphasis original).

---

[316] It 'occurs more than 250 times in Greek and Latin inscriptions' (Metzger 1994, 475).

[317] Declares Belleville (2005, 231): 'Church tradition from the Old Latin and Vulgate versions and early Greek and Latin fathers onwards affirms and lauds a female apostle. Yet modern scholarship has not been comfortable with the attribution . . . [A]n examination of primary usage in the computer databases of Hellenistic Greek literary works, papyri, inscriptions, and artifacts confirms . . . [Junia] and shows with ['chief among'] plus the plural dative bears without exception the inclusive sense "notable among".'

[318] For example, Browning (1997, 213); Bauckham (2002, 109-202).

[319] Witherington (2004, 399) conjectures that Junia may have been 'among those mentioned in 1 Cor. 15:7 as apostles to whom Christ appeared' and therefore an apostle in the primary sense.

[320] See, for example, Paul's OT citation in which he fleshes out 'daughters' 2 Cor. 6:18.

[321] The word 'brother' in the original is preceded by *tis* and clearly refers to either gender within the context. Sisters are not exempt from the strong censure. There are approximately 383 occurrences of this pronoun in the Greek New Testament, many of which are employed as interrogatives. The same inclusive idea is true of *pas* in 1 John 3:2: 'Everyone [*pas*] who has this hope in him purifies himself, just as he is pure'. Clearly, the 'everyone' in this context does not exclude the sisters, notwithstanding the masculine gender of *pas*. The feminine, interestingly, is *pasa-pasa* (making room for my 'stammering').

[322] And even in some cases such as 1Cor. 5:11 (see above) it is generic.

[323] Here, interestingly, the KJV 'man or woman'!

[324]'The little evidence we do have implies that heads of households from the earliest converts were normally appointed to such positions' (Acts 14: 23; 1 Cor. 1:16 and 16: 15-16)' (p.79).

[325] For example, only the Ephesian-Laodicean churches are given instructions concerning love of spouses and children (Eph. 5: 25; Col. 3:19; Tit. 2:4); only the Corinthians are rebuked for their abuse of tongues, etc.

[326] For study of this term, see Baldwin (1995, 65-80).

[327] Again, when the Ephesian believers first heard that the ascended Lord gave gifts to humankind (Eph. 4: 11ff), in terms of apostles . . . .pastors and teachers, they in all likelihood would have understood that these 'offices' were not limited to men, simply because the plurals are gender inclusive like the 'all' of Rom. 3: 23.

[328] See especially Piper and Grudem (1991).

[329] According to Waters (2004, 734) '"Childbearing in 1 Tim 2:15 is . . . metaphor for "virtue-bearing." . . . *All women and men* [particularly leaders] *must give birth to and continue in faith, love, holiness, and temperance in order to be saved.*' His italics.

[330] Smalley (1991, xxxiii); Westcott (xxxii). Says Irenaeus: 'Now the church at Ephesus was founded by Paul, but John stayed there until the times of Trajan . . .' (Cited in Eusebius 1926, 243).

[331] Based upon the hermeneutical canon: 'If the plain sense makes sense, seek no other sense, lest you end up with nonsense.' Grassmick (1974, 12) calls this principle the 'Plain meaning'.

[332332332] kuria (verses 1, 5). 'From ancient times opinion has been divided as to whether this letter was addressed to an anonymous noble lady, though she might have actually been called "Electa" (from the Gk. *Ekleka,* "chosen"), as Clement of Alexandra supposed, or even "Kyria" (a direct transliteration from the Gk. *Kyria,* "lady"), or whether it was addressed to a Christian community metaphorically identified as "the chosen lady and her children." Some commentators (. . . Ryrie) favour a person as the designee, while other commentators (. . . Bruce, Marshall, Stott, . . .) favour a local church' (Barker 1981, 361).

APPENDIX 10

Luke's Christmas Lyrics

"JIIZAS A-GO BAAN"

JAMIEKAN TEXT	ENGLISH TRANSLATION (NKJV)
XII. Song: Ilizibet (soprano), orchestra	Luke 1:42-45
Yu bles uman dan aal ada uman an di pikni we yu beh bles tu. 43Az mi bles so, dat di mada a mi Laad kom lok tu mi? 44Az ya taak so, braps! mi biebi jomp ina mi beli kaaz mi api. 45Yu bles kaaz yo biliiv wa di Laad se a-go apm.	42Blessed are you among women, and blessed is the fruit of your womb? 43But why is this granted to me, that the mother of my Lord should come to me? 44For indeed, as soon as the voice of your greeting sounded in my ears, the babe leaped in my womb for joy. 45Blessed is she who believed, for there will be a fulfillment of those things which were told her from the Lord."
XIII. Hymn: Choir, orchestra Text by Andrew Marshall	
1. Mieri, wat a Gad bles uman yu a; Fi a kyari im onggl bwau chil, Jiizas! Wat a swiit pitti-nem, no mis, Yes, is Gad wid us fi aal tim. *Gloria in excelsis deo.*	1. Mary, what a God blessed woman you are to carrying God's only Son, Jesus! what a sweet name indeed. g-Yes, it's God with us for all time. *Gloria in excelsis deo.*
2. Joyous was di song Ilizibet sang! Aal di biebi a jump, im glad tu. Dis bwaai Im kyan klens, purj, fri man fram sin. Im kyan mek everibadi bran niyuu. *Gloria in excelsis deo.*	2. Joyous was the song Elizabeth sang, even the baby jumped when he heard, he was so happy. This Child, He can cleanse, purge, and free men from sin. He can make everyone brand new. *Gloria in excelsis deo.*
3. Kom non, mek wi priez, give tanks to di Laad, Fi di koming of Krais di Saovya. Profets lang ago did tel of his bort, Non im kom an wiil liv fi eva. *Gloria in excelsis deo.*	3. Come now, let us praise God and thank Him for the coming of Christ the Saviour. Prophets long ago foretold his birth. Now He's here, and He will live forever. *Gloria in excelsis deo.*
The Song of Mary	
XIV. Song: Choir, Mieri (mezzo-soprano), orchestra Luke 1:46-55	
46Mieri se "Mi priez di Laad wid aal mi aat; 47mi soul priez Gad se siev mi. 48kaaz im si an memba mi im puor sorvant. Fram non aan, evri jenirieshan a-go se sa a Gad bles uman; 49kaaz di Muos Powaful Gad du da muukl ya fi mi. Im nieli! 50Gad gud ikyalo dem, an kain tu evribadi. ima evri jenirieshan we traiek tu priez im. 51Im tek an an di son powaful sitn im sky ata siyata luosa pupl. 52Gad aal dong puda eeta dem pon chruon, an lif op pupl we nobodi mean tingk se mata. 53Im gi ongle pupl nof op a gud sitn, bot rich pupl im sen we wid dem han langa yo. 54Gad elp mi sorvant dem, Izrel. Im memba ti to gud an kain tu dem 55jos lok os im did pramis Jebrayam an au pikni dem. Fi hi glad an kain tu dem fi eva."	46And Mary said: "My soul magnifies the Lord, 47And my spirit has rejoiced in God my Savior. 48For He has regarded the lowly state of His maidservant. For behold, henceforth all generations will call me blessed. 49For He who is mighty has done great things for me. And holy is His name. 50And His mercy is on those who fear Him From generation to generation. 51He has shown strength with His arm; He has scattered the proud in the imagination of their hearts. 52He has put down the mighty from their thrones. And exalted the lowly. 53He has filled the hungry with good things, And the rich He has sent away empty. 54He has helped His servant Israel, In remembrance of His mercy, 55As He spoke to our fathers, To Abraham and to his seed forever."

"JIIZAS A GO BAAN"

JAMIEKAN TEXT	ENGLISH TRANSLATION (NKJV)
Christ Born of Mary	
XV. **Recitative**: Narrator, continuo.	Luke 2:1-7
Iina dem die de, di Ruoman ruula, Siiza Agostos, gi aada fi rait dong di niem a evribadi iina im kindom. 2(Dis a di fos taim niem a rait dong sins di taim wen Kiriniyos did a ruul uova Siriya.) 3Aal im piipl dem did afi go a di toun we dem baan fi get dem niem rait dong, so di govament kyan taks dem. 4So kaaz Juozif did kom fram Dievid fambili an Dievid did baan iina Judiya, im did afi lef fram Nazaret iina Gyalalii an go a Betliyem iina Judiya. 5Juozif go de wid Mieri fi get dem niem rait dong. Di tuu a dem did ingiej fi marid dem wan aneda an shi did av biebi iina beli. 6Wen dem de de, Mieri tek iin fi av biebi, 7an shi av ar fos pikni, wan bwai. Shi rap im op iina biebi blangkit an put im iina di baks we di animal dem nyam outa, kaaz no spies neva iina di ges ous fi dem.	And it came to pass in those days *that* a decree went out from Caesar Augustus that all the world should be registered. ² This census first took place while Quirinius was governing Syria. ³ So all went to be registered, everyone to his own city. ⁴ Joseph also went up from Galilee, out of the city of Nazareth, into Judea, to the city of David, which is called Bethlehem, because he was of the house and lineage of David, ⁵ to be registered with Mary, his betrothed ⁽ᵃ⁾wife, who was with child. ⁶ So it was, that while they were there, the days were completed for her to be delivered. ⁷ And she brought forth her firstborn Son, and wrapped Him in swaddling cloths, and laid Him in a manger, because there was no room for them in the inn.
XVI. **Song** (No spies neva de de): Narrator, ienjel, choir, orchestra.	Text by Andrew Marshall
Dem did travl fram far, wid a lot of ope in dere harts, But wen dem finali riich, Dem almos sliip pon di street. Kaaz no spies neva deh deh fi ous di yung bwai, Jiizas; no spies neva deh deh fi Krais fi lay his swiit ed. Rapt in swaddilin klose, Jiizas di baan lang ago, Iina bax we di cow dem nyam outa. Mi neva know se di King cud de bout ya! Oh no! Kaaz no spies neva deh deh fi ous di yung bwai, Jiizas; no spies neva deh deh fi Krais fi lay his swiit ed. Di iin was full, not an empty room to spare, dem mus did hol dem one anada closely, dem mus did affa up a prayer.	They had traveled from far with a lot of hope in their hearts; but when they finally arrived, they almost slept on the streets, because there was no space there to make Jesus comfortable. No space was there for Christ to rest his sweet head. Wrapped in swaddling clothes, Jesus was born a long time ago in a box where the animals ate from; I didn't know a King could be in such a place, not at all! Because there was no space there to make Jesus comfortable. No space was there for Christ to rest his sweet head. The inn was full and there were no rooms to spare. They must have held each other closely, they must have offered up a prayer
Glory to God in the Highest	
XVII. **Recitative**: Narrator, continuo.	Luke 2:8-10
8Da nait de, som shepad did a luk aafa dem shiip iina wan fiil, mier we Mieri dem did de. 9Wan a di Laad ienjel dem kom tu di shepad dem. Wan brait brait lait fram Gad kova dem an it mek dem fraitn so til. 10So di ienjel tel dem se,	⁸ Now there were in the same country shepherds living out in the fields, keeping watch over their flock by night. ⁹ And behold, an angel of the Lord stood before them, and the glory of the Lord shone around them, and they were greatly afraid. ¹⁰ Then the angel said to them,

GRATEFUL ACKNOWLEDGMENTS

Pastor Andre Crouch of blessed memory has taught us to sing, *How Can I Say Thanks*…! His song was undoubtedly inspired by that wonderful anthem of gratitude (Psalm 103) that itemizes a myriad of blessings for which to praise the LORD—chief of which is the forgiveness of sins, followed by health and wellness.

In this regard the song writer's focus was on the one Supreme Being, who in Acts has been revealed to us as Son, Father, and Spirit (Acts 1). My debt of gratitude for the completion of this commentary follows suit.

On the horizontal level, I thank my ever-patient publisher for her wisdom and skill that go way beyond her youthful years. I'm also grateful to the staff and students of the CGST and the JTS as well as the Patti Care Group that nurtured me for the better part of twenty-five years, for their never ceasing encouragement to write clearly, properly and with conviction. One day their prayers will be answered.

Finally, my greatest debt of gratitude on this terrestrial level goes to the one who prays with and for me daily, and who prefers to remain anonymous. Thanks Babes!

O yes! How could I forget? I want to thank God for my fingers. I can always count on *dem.*

BIBLIOGRAPHY

Baldwin, Clinton. *Methods of Biblical Interpretation.* Spanish Town, JA: DP, 2012.

Barrett, C. K. *A Critical and Exegetical Commentary on the Acts of the Apostles*, 2 vols. Edinburgh: T & T Clark, 1994-98.

Bauer, W., et al. *A Greek-English Lexicon of the New Testament and Other Early Christian Literature.* Chicago: Chicago University Press, 2000.

Beekman, John, and J. Callow. *Translating the Word of God.* Grand Rapids: Zondervan, 1974.

Black, David. *Paul: Apostle of Weakness.* New York: Peter Lang, 1984.

_____. *Linguistics and New Testament Interpretation: Essays on Discourse Analysis.* Nashville: Broadman Press, 1984.

Black, Napoleon. *The Crucified Life.* Kingston: EMI, 2019.

Blass, F., et al. *A Greek Grammar of the New Testament and Other Early Christian Literature.* Chicago: Chicago University Press, 1961.

Bock, Darrell L. *Acts*. Grand Rapids: Baker, 2007.

Boring, Eugene M., et al. *Hellenistic Commentary to the New Testament*. Nashville: Abingdon, 1995.

Bosch, David J. *Transforming Mission: Paradigm Shifts in Theology of Mission*. Maryknoll, New York: Orbis, 1991.

Bruce, F. F. *The Acts of the Apostles*. 2nd edition. London: Tyndale, 1952.

Campbell, Sheldon, "Calvinistic Baptists in Jamaica? A Historical-theological Study of the Relationship among the Theology and Work of Five Pioneering Missionaries in Jamaica." Doctoral Dissertation, Stellenbosch University, 2020.

Chisholm, Clinton. *A Controversial Clergyman*. Kingston: EMI, 2019.

Cooke, L. *The Story of Jamaican Missions: How the Gospel Went from Jamaica to the World*. Kingston: Arawak, 2013.

Conzelmann, Hans. *Acts of the Apostles*. Philadelphia: Fortress, 1987.

Dunn, James. *Baptism in the Holy Spirit*, Philadelphia: Westminster, 1977.

Escobar, Samuel. *A Time for Mission*. Leicester: Langham, 2003.

Fernando, Ajith, et al. *Acts: The Message of Jesus in Action*. Grand Rapids: Zondervan, 2010.

Gaventa, Beverly. *Acts*. Nashville: Abingdon, 2003.

―――――. 'Theology and Ecclesiology in the Miletus Speech: Reflections on Content and Context,' *NTS* 50 (2004):36-52.

Grudem, Wayne. *The Gift of Prophecy in 1 Corinthians*. Washington: University Press of America, 1982.

Keener, Craig S. *Acts: An Exegetical Commentary*, 4 vols. Grand Rapids: Baker, 2012-15.

―――――. *Acts*. Cambridge: CUP, 2020.

Lofthouse, W. F. "I and We in the Pauline Letters," ET 64 (1952) 242-245.

Metzger, Bruce M. "The Formulas Introducing Quotations of Scripture in the New Testament and the Mishnah," JBL 70 (1951) 297–307.

―――――. *A Textual Commentary on the Greek New Testament*. Stuttgart: Deutsche Bibelgesellschaft, 1994.

Middleton, J Richard. *A New Heaven and a New Earth: Reclaiming Biblical Eschatology*. Grand Rapids: Baker, 2014.

Nicholson, C. *Baptism: Let's not Water it Down*! North Charleston, SC: CreateSpace, 2016.

Owen, Samuel. "Evangelism: Theology, Methods and Message." *AJET* 13 (1994) 86–116.

Palmer, D. V., "I-n-I in the NT and the Hermeneutics of Caribbean Theology," Groundings: Catholic Theological Reflections on Issues Facing Caribbean People in the 21st Century 29 (2013): 37-59.

———."The Messianic Community and Christian Mission." Paper for the 71st General Meeting of SNTS, Montreal, Canada, Seminar 6 "The Mission and Expansion of Earliest Christianity," August, 2016.

———. "Lukan Literary Strategy and Soteriology as Public Theology," *CJET* 19 (2020): 64-77.

———. 'Lukan Historiography and Caribbean Theology' in *Contending Voices in Caribbean Theology,* eds. Judith Soares and Oral Thomas. Kingston: Jugaro, 2019.

———. "Chiastic Contours and the Book of Acts," *CJET* 17 (2018): 94-112.

———, and Samantha Mosha. *New Testament Theology: Identity & I-deology*. Kingston: EMI, 2019.

Pao, David. *Acts and the Isaianic New Exodus*. Eugene, OR: Wipf & Stock, 2000.

Peterson, David G. *The Acts of the Apostles*. Grand Rapids: Eerdmans, 2009.

Ratzlaff, Dale. *Sabbath in Crisis.* Glendale, AZ: Life Assurance Ministries, 2003.

Richards, Jo-Ann Faith. *Godincidences: Adventuring with an Awesomely Sovereign, Sovereignly Awesome God.* Bloomington, Indiana: Author House, 2010.

Rienecker, Fritz. *Linguistic Key to the Greek New Testament.* Grand Rapids: Zondervan, 1980.

Robertson, A. T. *A Grammar of the Greek New Testament in the Light of Historical Research.* Nashville: Broadman, 1934.

Schnabel, Eckhard J. *Acts.* Grand Rapids: Zondervan, 2012.

Selassie, Haile. "Building an Enduring Tower." In *One Race, One Gospel, One Task*, edited by C. F. H. Henry and W. S. Mooneyham. Minneapolis: WWP, 1967.

Stewart, Donald K. *Purposeful Evangelism and Missions: Missing Dimensions.* Parker, CO: Outskirts Press, 2010.

Stott, John. *The Message of Acts.* Nottingham, IVP: 1984.

Taylor, Burchell. *The Church Taking Sides: A Contextual Reading of the Letters to the Seven Churches in the Book of Revelation.* Kingston, JA: BBC, 1995.

———. "Messianic Ideology and Caribbean Theology of Liberation." In *Chanting Down Babylon: The Rastafari Reader*, edited by Nathaniel Samuel Murrell, et al. Philadelphia: TUP, 1998.

Thompson, A.J. *The Acts of the Risen Lord Jesus*. Nottingham, IVP: 2011.

Turner, M. M. B. "Spiritual Gifts Then and Now." VE 15 (1985) 7–64.

Wedderburn, Taneika Diana. A Comparison of the Grammatico-historical and Socio-literary Hermeneutical Approaches to Understanding 'Legion' in Mark 5:1-20." CGST thesis, 2017.

_____."So What Went into the Pigs?" *Caribbean Journal of Evangelical Theology* 19 (2020): 64-87.

Witherington, Ben, III. *The Acts of the Apostles: A Socio-Rhetorical Commentary*. Grand Rapids: Eerdmans, 1998.

_____.Wright, N. T et al. *Acts*. Downers Grove, ILL: IVP, 2010.

Yorke, Gosnell. "Bible Translation in Anglophone Africa and Her Diaspora: A Postcolonialist Agenda." *Black Theology: An International Journal* 2: (2004) 153-166.

_____. "Jamaican Creole," in *A Guide to Bible Translation: People, Languages, Topics*. Maitland Fl.: Xulon/Swindon: UBS, 2019.

RESOURCES BY DELANO PALMER

Messianic 'I' and Rastafari in New Testament Dialogue: Bio-Narratives, the Apocalypse, and Paul's Letter to the Romans

New Testament Theology: Identity and I-deology

Romans in Context

Theology of the New Testament: A Postcolonial Perspective

ABOUT THE AUTHOR

DELANO VINCENT PALMER is the Scholar-in-Residence at the Caribbean Graduate School of Theology (CGST), with chief responsibility to promote research in Indigenous Religious Studies and encourage regional scholars to publish.

Dr. Palmer served as the Deputy President of the Jamaica Theological Seminary. He is a Bible Teacher in the Swallowfield Chapel's Adult Christian Education (ACE) programme and adjunct lecturer at the Jamaica Theological Seminary.

He holds membership in the following professional organizations: Society of Biblical Literature, Society of Caribbean Professors of Religious Studies, Studiorum Novi Testamenti Societas (SNTS), and is the co-author of *New Testament Theology: Identity & I-deology*.

www.ingramcontent.com/pod-product-compliance
Lightning Source LLC
Chambersburg PA
CBHW020351170426